THE NANCY PELOSI WAY

THE NANCY PELOSI WAY

ADVICE ON SUCCESS, LEADERSHIP, AND POLITICS FROM AMERICA'S MOST POWERFUL WOMAN

CHRISTINE PELOSI

Skyhorse Publishing

Skyhorse Publishing books may be purchased in bulk at special discounts for sales promotion, corporate gifts, fund-raising, or educational purposes. Special editions can also be created to specifications. For details, contact the Special Sales Department, Skyhorse Publishing, 307 West 36th Street, 11th Floor, New York, NY 10018 or info@skyhorsepublishing.com.

Skyhorse® and Skyhorse Publishing® are registered trademarks of Skyhorse Publishing, Inc.®, a Delaware corporation.

Visit our website at www.skyhorsepublishing.com.

10 9 8 7 6 5 4 3 2

Library of Congress Cataloging-in-Publication Data is available on file.

Cover design by Brian Peterson
Cover photo credit Getty Images

ISBN: 978-1-5107-5584-0
Ebook ISBN 978-1-5107-5585-7

Printed in the United States of America

Contents

"I really want women to know their power, to value their experience. To understand that nothing has been more wholesome in the political process than the increased involvement of women."

—House Speaker Nancy Pelosi

Introduction

On December 12, 2018, the nation held its collective breath as a bizarre scene unfolded on national television. President Donald Trump, Vice President Mike Pence, Senate Democratic Leader Charles Schumer, and House Democratic Leader Nancy Pelosi were in the Oval Office for what was supposed to be a meeting to avoid a federal government shutdown. Dressed in a green dress and seated poised on a chair facing the president as befits the leader of a coequal branch of government meeting at the White House, Pelosi saw the budget negotiations devolve into a barrage of interruptions, mansplaining, and third-party insults from the president, who was trying to needle her for not having 218 votes publicly announced in her bid to return as Speaker of the House.

Finally it came to this:

Trump: "Nancy's in a situation where it's not easy for her to talk right now, and I understand, and I fully understand that. We're going to have a good discussion, and we're going to see what happens. But we have to have border security."

Pelosi: "Mr. President—Mr. President, please don't characterize the strength that I bring to this meeting as the leader of the House Democrats, who just won a big victory."

In that moment, she obliterated any doubts about her resolve to return as Speaker with calm and confidence, or about her ability to corral an unruly president's out-of-control negotiations, or her intention to be a role model for girls told they didn't belong, professional women talked over by blustery men, and older women told they were no longer useful. A few moments later, having refused to fund a border wall for which the president had repeatedly said Mexico would pay, Nancy Pelosi pulled on a 2012 winter coat the designer had presciently named "red fire," slipped on her shades, and stepped out of the White House and into meme history.

The next day, she locked down her 218th vote and her historic position as the first and second woman Speaker of the House of Representatives.

That moment was chosen for this book cover because it encapsulates the Nancy Pelosi Way: a woman in full who knows the power of bringing her complete self—as a leader, as a political force, as a legislator, as an activist, as a mom, and as the daughter of a powerhouse mother whose dreams were ahead of her time—to the moment.

Suddenly the coat meme was everywhere: videos, fan art, campaign swag. I have the pillowcase to give my daughter a virtual confidence-building hug from her Mimi as needed, and definitely wear the shades pin for the boost.

How did this explode?

First, I think there are a lot of people who have always wanted to get in a room with the president of the United States and hold their own, regardless of party. As Nancy often says, you have to be able to "breathe the air at the highest altitudes." Many people—including presidents—forget themselves when they get to the Oval Office and need to be reminded that they are mortal. This particular denizen of the Oval Office—perhaps more than most—needed the reality check that he represents but one coequal branch of government. Rather than a sycophant whispering in his ear, Trump got a free and powerful woman telling him out loud in view and earshot of the cameras he himself had ushered in: "Remember, your presidency is mortal."

Second, after all the sexism and misogyny that was hurled at Nancy Pelosi and Hillary Clinton over the years and in the 2016 presidential campaign and then at Nancy Pelosi after Hillary lost, Nancy had the audacity to stay, while in the words of Joy Ann Reid, some people feel the need to "flee to the safety of a white male candidate." Certainly one had been offered—sort of. The goal of a small group of people in the House was to force out Nancy Pelosi; then, a new hypothetical safe candidate would emerge whom Republicans—who mercilessly attacked straight white male military veteran Democrats including Max Cleland, Tom Daschle, Al Gore, John Kerry, and Jack Murtha—would decide to leave alone. They continued on the path even after Nancy led the effort to win back the House Democratic majority, which is why Trump thought bullying Nancy about the speakership fight in public in the third person was somehow going to unnerve her. If a billion-dollar multiyear negative ad campaign from the far right and 137,000 negative ads against her in the 2018 campaign cycle had not fazed Nancy Pelosi, his remarks didn't stand a chance—except to boomerang. Which they did.

Third, Nancy Pelosi has a depth of experience and professionalism that is relatable for millions of career women who show up twice as prepared, coiffed, and focused as men only to be ignored, talked over, or co-opted when men steal their ideas right in front of them and receive rapturous praise for such "original" thinking. Maybe after two years of all the boorishness, we just wanted to see some joy in a woman comfortable in her power and ready to fight for it just like a man would—if in fact there would ever be a male party leader who would coach his team to victory and then get fired.

Naturally, as a daughter, I see things behind the scenes that others don't, so the purpose of this storytelling is to add context to the public stories that I think shaped

Nancy Pelosi as a daughter, mother, wife, friend, representative, and role model to aspiring leaders looking to step into their own power and make their own choices—not those dictated to them. I deliberately chose to tell a few stories of ways in which Nancy Pelosi was forged by childhood, school, and parenthood. I tell stories of her first campaign for Congress, her efforts to elect more women leaders (which has helped create the most diverse Congress in history, with thirty-five new women members elected in 2018, compared to the twelve House Democratic congresswomen who served together when she arrived in 1987), her innovative ways of getting her message to the people and the people's message to the Congress, and her latest campaign to protect her legislative baby, the Patient Protection and Affordable Care Act.

Her story is historic and unique, but I hope the lessons are universal.

1

Know Your Power

When Nancy Patricia D'Alesandro was a young girl growing up in Baltimore, political office was seen as the path for her five brothers, not their baby sister. Her mother was Nancy Lombardi D'Alesandro, an immigrant from Italy who married at nineteen and never again lived outside the Little Italy neighborhood of row houses, St. Leo's Catholic Church parish, Italian businesses, and Democratic precincts patrolled by the "moccasin army" she commanded for her husband, the New Deal congressman-turned-mayor Thomas D'Alesandro. "Big Tommy" and "Big Nancy" had seven children (one boy died as a small child) and a network of thousands of constituents who would drop in at all hours of the day or night to seek help, pay it forward, exchange political news, and build community power. More often than not, they were greeted at the door by "Little Nancy," the girl who would grow up to leave Baltimore for Trinity College in Washington, DC, and follow her college sweetheart Paul Pelosi to New York City, then to his hometown of San Francisco, where, after years of raising their five children (all born within six years and one week) and building community power herself, she would be elected to the Congress of the United States in 1987 and then elected by her colleagues to be the first (in 2007) and the second (in 2019) woman (and Italian American) Speaker of the House, and one of only a handful of people ever to return to the Speaker's Chair.

"I was born into a family that was devoutly Catholic, proud of our Italian American heritage, fiercely patriotic, and staunchly Democratic," Nancy often says. "That was our family. Our parents raised us to be proud of our Italian Catholic heritage, patriotic in our love of country, and respectful of the dignity and worth of every person. They taught us that we have responsibilities to each other, and that public service was a noble calling. We were always giving out buttons, placards, bumper stickers, and the rest. But we were first and foremost a family, even though my father was mayor. So it was Mayor outside, it was Daddy at home. There never was a time when you entered our home that, in the vestibule, there weren't buttons, placards, or stickers and the like for whatever the campaign was, whether it was presidential, gubernatorial, or local."

This long journey from answering the door at 245 Albemarle Street to answering the call to lead Congress was paved by hard work, deep faith, and the unerring ability to believe in her "why" over and over again, confounding the experts and expectations.

The first time she was elected to House leadership as Democratic Whip—October 10, 2001—a torrent of letters came from across America telling Nancy Pelosi that in her victory they saw their dreams: the unfulfilled dreams of elders who—like her own mother—had never been able to reach their professional goals—and the hopeful dreams of parents knowing that their daughters had a new role model who would pave the way for others. The most oft-received quote in the letters from people across the country was one Nancy used herself from Eleanor Roosevelt: "The future belongs to those who believe in the beauty of their dreams." Eleanor Roosevelt was a contemporary of Nancy D'Alesandro. Tommy was a New Deal congressman and big supporter of President Franklin Roosevelt (so much so that he named a son after FDR and supported him in most politics with major exceptions being the treatment of refugees and the need for the creation of a Jewish homeland). But like many women of that generation, Nancy D'Alesandro did not make it beyond Little Italy. She raised her family at 245 Albemarle Street; her parents lived at 235 Albemarle while her in-laws lived at 204. She was a member of the Women's Democratic Club in Washington, DC, where Eleanor Roosevelt did her radio addresses. She was an

inventor and an organizer, and even matriculated at
Maryland Law School, but never completed her studies
after her young son died. Years later, when I passed the
California bar exam, I mailed her an invitation and she
wrote back saying: "I am the second happiest person to
receive this notice from the Bar Examiners. How happy I
am to see you accomplish what I could not 55 years ago."
Her dreams of professional success were in her daughter
and later her granddaughters. But her energy was in running the campaigns and serving constituents out of the
family home and training her daughter to respect people
and serve them. As first lady of Baltimore, my grandmother actively used her platform to improve housing in
the city. She showed Nancy what a significant role women
could play in politics as she worked hand in hand with
her husband to serve the people of Baltimore. But political
ambitions—running for office or serving in a government
job—were reserved for the men until Nancy paved her
own path to Congress and then to leadership that honored
the beauty of the dreams of those early women leaders.

But to win leadership, Nancy had to run, and when
she announced her intentions in 2000, the first question
some of her as-yet-unenlightened Democratic congressional colleagues asked was, "Who said she could run?"
Nancy's reaction: "Oh really? I have to have your permission to run? You have really stoked my fire—now
I'm definitely running if you think I have to have your
permission!"

Yes, they really asked, "Who said she could run?"

Why? Because they'd had a pecking order for the over two hundred years since the Founders, of white man to white man to white man—and they mentored these men and gave them perks and positions to cultivate the loyalties they would need to succeed. What they had not counted on was a woman stepping forward. To Pelosi supporters, Nancy was a successful California Democratic Party chair, master legislator on the Appropriations Committee and Select Permanent Committee on Intelligence, and longtime campaigner who knew how to win elections and elect diverse people who fit their districts and could deliver results. To the status quo, she was an interloper cutting in line and challenging corporate structural power with legions of grassroots donors large and small. So little did they think of congresswomen as potential party leaders that with the exception of her mock swearing-in in a ceremonial room, the first time Nancy Pelosi entered the Democratic Speaker's office for a meeting was as the Democratic Speaker.

So they did what power does, and attempted to appease the competition by co-opting the situation. Some party elders came to Nancy and said, in effect, "We see that you have a lot of support from women. Why don't you women give us a list of the things you want done and we will get them done for you?" Her reaction: "Those poor babies. I don't think so!" They had no idea what they were dealing with. Women don't want men to lead for us—we want to lead on the strength of our own ideas and talents at building coalitions to turn ideas into

laws. We are not running as women—we *are* women—
we are running as leaders who can bring our skills and
experiences to the table for everyone. Besides, how would
men help women achieve their financial, education, and
professional equality if they did the work for them?

Every time I deconstruct that story I can't help but
wonder: Were there women before who gave them the
list? Who quietly subsumed their ideas to get something
done? This wasn't a new trick trotted out to appease
Nancy Pelosi and eliminate her as a threat; this was a
practiced move. And that's why so many women and
men found it enraging. Attempts at co-option and fla-
grant condescension only made Nancy more determined
to run and to win, not because she was a woman (in
which case she likely would have lost), but because she
could lead the caucus of mostly men to vote for her and
unite around her leadership.

Nancy's argument about why she should become the
most powerful woman in Congress was less to do with
gender than it was to do with direction: that a daughter of
the New Deal would shape the course of the Democratic
Party by echoing FDR's call for "bold persistent exper-
imentation." At the time Washington Democrats were
in a battle of influence between the business-oriented
Democratic Leadership Council and the base constituencies of women, communities of color, LGBTQ
Americans, organized labor, civil rights campaigners, and
environmental activists. At the time that some wanted to
compromise with President George W. Bush on a second

round of tax cuts, Nancy insisted that government needed to work for the people and help them with jobs, health care, housing, and equal rights. Most important to her colleagues interested in winning back the House, Nancy had led the campaign to flip four California seats from Republican to Democratic.

When Nancy won as House Democratic Whip, she said "We have made history—now we must make progress!" But she had barely finished saying that to the press before a male reporter cut her off—at her victory press conference. Would he have interrupted a male whip? A question for the ages, and a sign of things to come. But regardless of how obviously some people clearly needed to get used to a woman in power, Nancy won and she was ready to lead.

Being the first woman to lead a political party in Congress (as Leader and Speaker) gave Nancy the opportunity to celebrate other trailblazing women. She has held Women's History Month events to honor women veterans; women mathematicians of America's space program; Supreme Court justices; and other women congressional leaders like her friend Lindy Boggs, who once told Nancy when Nancy was concerned that she had perhaps too many titles at one time—chairing the 1984 convention host committee, the delegate selection committee, and the California Democratic Party—"Darling, no man would have ever said that. And so, darling, know thy power and use it."

When Nancy wrote her bestselling book, she used the title *Know Your Power*. Lindy knew hers. One day she,

Nancy, Barbara Boxer, and other congresswomen went over to the Senate to protest the Republican Senate's efforts to disallow a vote on the Civil Rights Act amendment in 1990. A Republican senator from Minnesota was incredibly rude, telling them, "You don't belong here." When the congresswomen said they were members of Congress with floor privileges, he said, "Oh, I thought you were staff," (as if that made his rudeness any more acceptable) and pushed the congresswomen off to the side. But the women refused to be treated that way: they talked to the press and they were very clear that they did belong there, not only because members of Congress have House floor privileges and Senate floor privileges, but also morally, that women have a right to be present. They were literally told to go to the side and be quiet—and that led to the Republican's defeat as a senator against Paul Wellstone in the next election and started the congresswomen on a path that ended up with Boxer being a senator, Boggs being an ambassador to the Vatican, and Nancy being Speaker of the House.

The lesson: Know your power and use it. Do not confine yourself to other people's expectations for you and make conscious decisions to put girls and women in the position of developing and knowing their power. If Nancy had listened to what 1950s Baltimore expected of her, her life would have been very different. Had she listened to the people who asked for her "list," she never would have shown herself and others that women do not have to wait our turn (that may never come) and settle for derivative power instead of elected power. But she made the choice to break up the pecking order and refused to be treated as "less than." And as Nancy's story illustrates, you don't want to be pigeonholed as "running as a woman." Instead, remind people that you are running as the best person for the job. There is a fine line between empowering a different kind of leadership and collaborative skills people expect from women versus making gender the sole rationale (as opposed to one of the benefits) of your candidacy. Fight to earn power because you are a leader, not because it is "your turn."

What is true in politics is true across the professions. Little girls are still not encouraged to pursue the hard sciences, young women are underrepresented in STEM or STEAM (Science, Technology, Engineering, Arts, and Math). And while more women jumped into politics in 2017 like never before, we still have vast underrepresentation at the highest levels.

Women need to lead, and other women need to support them. Too often there is a scarcity argument—that, like crabs in a barrel, only one can rise to the top by climbing over the others. Sometimes it's described as the "woman's seat" on a board or commission or legislative slate, as if there can only be one.

When there is only one woman, she has to be the only everything—the only woman/person of color/person with a disability/LGBTQ person/the only other everything other than white men who aren't expected to carry the dreams of others who never made it to the table. It is sadly still too common even in "progressive" or "meritocratic" spaces to hear "I'm the first woman in my family to graduate from law school, so I don't have a role model for being in court" or "I'm the only openly gay person on my board" or "I'm the only young person on my leadership team" or "Tell me about it, I'm the only woman and only person of color so they think they've got a twofer" or "They say tech is a meritocracy, but 'bro-grammers' are as sexist as *Mad Men*[1]." We who have been "the only one" know what it's like to engage with people who did not grow up in a just society and are adapting to women, people of color, and LGBTQ Americans in positions of leadership. To be asked "Is your boss here yet?" or "Can you grab us some coffee while you're up?" or "My wife would love your dress." We know what it's like when people shake your white male assistant's hand, assuming he is your supervisor. We know what it's like to suggest an idea, only to hear it echoed by a man, and then hear the group praise the man for "his" idea. We are pleasantly surprised when given credit for our own ideas in real time. We know what it's like facing *Mad Men* mores and earning *Mad Men* paychecks.

There is little hope of escaping sexism considering that *to this very day* men talk over Speaker Nancy Pelosi. We saw it ourselves on camera in the Oval Office in December 2018. We read about it a year before when Nancy was at an informal White House dinner with the president, Leader Schumer, and various administration

---

1   A show about advertising set in the 1950s.

officials trying to make a deal on DACA. At one point, Commerce Secretary Wilbur Ross asked, "What exactly does the president get out of this deal?" Nancy, the only woman at the table out of eleven people, started to answer, but the men in the room began talking over her and one another. Exasperated, Nancy asked, "Do the women get to talk around here?" As a reporter put it: "There was, at last, silence, and she was not interrupted again."[2]

And Nancy has seen it with men who come to Washington to ask Congress for help and treat her with chauvinism and talk to the men around her but not to her. At the 2004 convention, Nancy went to practice the speech she would give as the House Democratic Leader, laying out the vision and agenda on which presidential nominee Senator John Kerry and every candidate for Congress would run. A man assigned to prep with her said, "Okay, now let's work on your tone to match Mrs. Heinz Kerry, who is giving her speech in a certain tone"—to which Nancy said, "With respect to Mrs. Kerry, I'm giving my speech as a congressional leader, not as a wife." There are some hapless souls who still treat Nancy that way during her second term of service as Speaker of the House. They are completely uncomfortable with women in power. You would think they would have aides who would say "You should really look the Speaker of the House in the eye when

2   Ashley Parker, "Trump and Democrats Strike DACA Deal. Yes? No? Sort of? Trump's World Can Be Confusing," *Washington Post*, September 14, 2017, https://www.washingtonpost.com/politics/trump-and-democrats-strike-daca-deal-yes-no-sort-of-trumps-world-can-be-confusing/2017/09/14/ab6a40d4-9970-11e7-82e4-f1076f6d6152_story.html

you talk to her," if only for practical political reasons—but, alas, you would be wrong. But Nancy doesn't let that stop her: she takes note, and she goes around them, knowing her power and showing her "why." And she rededicates herself to bringing more quality and equality to leadership.

The numbers matter: one diverse person is alone and the only everything other. Two diverse people are pitted against each other; three is a critical mass. That's when change can happen; that's when people can start to have the confidence to demand policies that are more authentic and representative. Studies show that gender diversity enhances the bottom line.[3] The more diverse a team is, the more likely it is to make the best business decision, because multiple perspectives add authenticity and avoid groupthink. A 2017 *Forbes* study of six hundred business decisions made by two hundred different teams over a two-year span found that more diverse and inclusive teams made better decisions up to 87 percent of the time, took less time to make the decision, and delivered 60 percent better results.[4] Credit Suisse found that boards with more women had a 36 percent higher return on equity.[5]

The #MeToo Movement showed us how many

3 Jeff Desjardins, "How Gender Diversity Enhances the Bottom Line," *Visual Capitalist*, January 23, 2018, https://www.visualcapitalist.com/gender-diversity-bottom-line/.

4 Erik Larson, "New Research: Diversity + Inclusion = Better Decision Making at Work," *Forbes*, September 21, 2017, https://www.forbes.com/sites/eriklarson/2017/09/21/new-research-diversity-inclusion-better-decision-making-at-work/#281ff9544cbf.

5 Ian Kar, "Companies with More Women Directors Generate a 36% Higher Return on Equity," *Quartz*, December 7, 2015, https://qz.com/566977/companies-with-more-women-directors-generate-a-36-higher-return-on-equity/.

women found their calling and tried to develop their power but were harassed out of opportunities to advance professionally. When the We Said Enough/Me Too Politics advocacy reached Congress, Nancy convened congresswomen and stakeholders to support a change to the capitol culture. Representative Jackie Speier's bipartisan reforms changed the rules by which Congress conducts itself. This was a tough time—there were popular members who faced reckonings for past behavior. In one instance, the five days it took Nancy to successfully call on one long-serving member with a secret sexual harassment settlement to step aside seemed like agony at the time—with Nancy attacked for saying there should be due process for accuser and accused. But as it turned out, insisting on a process that would be fair and setting forth a structure and a standard meant that members knew the standards by which they would be judged. By contrast, it took the Senate twenty-one days from accusations to resignation of a popular senator, and many people still feel that was far too rushed. Charting a fair course forward while dealing with multiple opinions and varied situations required a thick skin and a deft touch. Most people agreed that something had to be done, but they disagreed on the how and the why and the when. Nancy and House Democrats moved swiftly to change their internal caucus rules and to roil through some tough changes and departures, but had to wait another year before the Senate acted on bicameral reforms that affected both chambers.

Cleaning up one's own house is not often easy, but it is often necessary to usher in respect, inclusivity, and dignity—and to hardwire those values into campaigns and legislative offices. This in turn creates more confidence that women, people of color, and LGBTQ Americans know their power to make decisions and policies more authentic and equitable.

And there is a new partnership in attacking and dismantling the world of the old bulls. In conversation onstage at the IGNITE/Running Start's Young Women Run conference in July 2017, I asked about a comment an old bull had made when she first became Whip: "Nancy will be a great leader—she can even be Speaker—she just needs to look out for old bulls and jealous women." She said, "That was a while ago—women now—young women understand that this is not a zero-sum game—if you succeed, she can succeed. It just gets bigger and bigger. The more women succeed, the more women succeed. There was an older notion of if you get it than I won't get it kind of thing. I think that notion is diminishing now." Her advice to overcome the sexism and scarcity arguments: "Know your power. Give yourself credit for what you have done—even if, like me, it was being home taking care of the family—one of the most important jobs in the country. Don't let anyone have a mystique—they went to that school, they are wearing that tie. The new gold standard is you. Let them measure up to what you are."

When you think of yourself as the new gold standard for public service, *that's* knowing your power.

2

Proper Preparation Prevents Poor Performance

To a young mother of five children—Nancy was thirty when she brought home her youngest child Alexandra, the week after her eldest, Nancy Corinne, turned six— time management was everything. Methodically planning each troop movement with precision and diplomacy was vital to the stability, ethos, and growth of the family. Growing up in a large family imbued an ethic of cooperation and coordination, but Nancy was far from home and the immediate bonds of family when she and Paul had four children in New York City before moving to San Francisco in 1969. Pregnant for most of the sixties, she piled one, two, then three children in a stroller to visit the parks of New York City and—during campaign season—to volunteer in get-out-the-vote efforts. Years later, when I wrote my first *Campaign Boot Camp* book, I asked how she got past the "No Solicitation" signs. "I was a mom with three babies in a stroller—who was going to stop me?" she replied. Who indeed?

When her children were young, she dressed everyone alike—identical skirts for Nancy, Jacqueline, Alexandra, and me with the color-coordinated pants for my brother Paul.

She would take the clothes out of the dryer and they would all be in a pile. Then the kids would come, and each would pull out what he or she wanted and fold those pieces in an individual stack. She might say, "Okay, everyone, white pants and yellow turtleneck"; then there would be a race to the laundry room because with everyone being relatively close in age and size, the first one would get the best clothes and the last might have a grass stain or frayed hole to contend with.

Each day began the night before, when she would prepare dinner while checking on homework and house-work; press the girls' Catholic school uniforms and super-vise the polishing of our white shoes; clean the dinner plates while setting out bowls for breakfast; make sure we had our baths and cuddle us in the towels, saying, "Got to keep my babies warm"; then send us off with "Goodnight, God bless you, pleasant dreams," and we would reply "Goodnight Jesus; thank you for everything; God bless everyone; amen." As the morning broke there were breakfasts to serve while lining up ten pieces of wheat bread, lunch meats, apples, and snacks assembly-line style so that we could make our lunches before heading to school. To this day, we rarely finish eating one meal without planning the next.

She would line up the four girls and pull our hair into two very tight braids each. My dad would try to help get us out the door, but when it came to hair he was a softie and the girl with the dad braids would have ponytails by the time she got to the first of the two buses we took to get to school. Nancy wore striped "Terrific" brand T-shirts with solid pants. She wore her hair long and straight— watching us didn't give her much time for fashion, much less time for even washing her face on the busiest days, though she occasionally went to a very groovy hair salon with a bead curtain and soul music to get coiffed and transformed. We tried to walk in her platform shoes and dress up in her clothes, but for the most part we laughed at her "mom clothes" until they became trendy later and we begged to borrow them.

Growing up, we spent most days at the playground in San Francisco's Presidio—then still a military base that the Army would transfer to the Parks Service under a bill written by Phil Burton in the 1970s. In the 1990s, Nancy would lead the fight with Dianne Feinstein and Barbara Boxer to save the Presidio from being sold off to private developers—but that was a lifetime away. As children we played, and Nancy would track all five of us in various play structures, listening for signs of distress and ignoring drama with a shrug unless someone was actually injured. She had a keen sense of who needed attention and who needed to be left alone. With five kids there are always coalition dynamics in play, so she would usually wait out an argument before stepping in. Her bits of advice that began as the "momily" are now known to her grandchildren as the collection of Mimi-isms. On fighting: "You play rough, you get hurt." On teasing each other: ignore that person. "Don't take the bait. Never." On family competitions in cards and backgammon: "First you need to learn how to play the game. Then you need to learn how to win the game." On going out wearing a slobby outfit: "What are you saving your good clothes for?" On using bad manners, instead of asking "where are your manners?" she says: "Could you pretend that you are at a polite dinner party?" On arguing: "You don't always have to set the world straight. You can be right but you don't always need to gloat about it. There's a better way to say it in a nicer way." On luck: "There is no luck. The harder I work, the luckier I get." On keeping secrets: "I'm a member of the MYOB (Mind Your Own Business) Club. Nobody knows what I have in my pocket." On dating: "Never say no—he might have cute friends," and the ultimate: "Never date a cheap man—if he's cheap with his money, he's cheap with his emotions, and he's cheap with his love." On betrayal: "He loved you—but he loved himself more."

As in politics, where Nancy says, "Be your own authentic self"—around the family she would say, "Be responsible for your own self. Your grades are your grades and they may vary from other people's. You each have different talents and your parents don't compare you to each other." The corollary to that was if someone got into trouble and the others were too gleeful, the others would get into even more trouble for gossiping. She would give us trouble for getting a sibling in trouble and say "Don't be a Mister or Miss Make-Matters-Worse." She tried to get us to keep each other's confidences and to not judge each other. She was present in the moment and kept a watchful eye.

In 1977, Nancy was elected Northern Chair of the California Democratic Party and started traveling thousands of miles around the state to visit local Democrats. The five kids would pile in the Jeep Wagoneer with her and travel from the redwoods up north to the raisin fields of the Central Valley to the vineyards and veterans' home in Napa to the various parades and festivals in the big cities and small towns. We cheered on the jumping frogs of Calaveras County—a tradition that Mark Twain had popularized in his short story a century before—decorated shrunken Styrofoam hats in a village near Lake Tahoe, and survived a harrowing car accident en route to the Garamendi family's annual Basque barbeque in Stockton, when the Jeep flipped over several times, but my dad got all seven of us out safely.

At home she was constantly on the phone. She raised money for Democratic candidates and voter registration drives, constantly calling up people and talking about the issues while we did our homework. All the kids stuffed and sealed envelopes, sorted mail pieces by zip code for mailing, passed the canapés, and got to know the hundreds of people who came through our home, which was used for fund-raisers and friend-raisers. Senator Alan Cranston would come for events and get all the kids to lace up and jog with him beforehand—he had buttons for all that said I RAN WITH SENATOR CRANSTON. When Governor Jerry Brown first came to the house, his gift buttons read IF YOU THINK EDUCATION IS EXPENSIVE, TRY IGNORANCE. He would go running alone, then use the rooms upstairs to shower and change—which the kids thought was cool until the day he outed us by coming downstairs and asking Nancy, "What's the name of your cat?" She didn't know we had a cat secretly living in the attic—and after that we didn't. The then bachelor governor once took a look at the well-worn, formerly white couch in the kitchen and said, "This is too far gone— you should just cover it." Nancy would often retell the story, saying, "You know you've been spending too much time in politics when you're getting home decorating tips from Jerry Brown."

Many of those grassroots events were designed to welcome Volunteers In Politics—the true VIPs—into the Democratic Party community. They helped win elections and formed the grassroots army that registered one million voters across the state when Nancy was state chair. At some point in 1982, amid inviting the 1984 Democratic presidential candidates to the state convention, Nancy decided to put in a bid to host the national convention. The community events that had begun as a partisan way to build up the party became part of a nonpartisan effort to bring the convention to the city.

A 1984 *New York Times* profile by Anne-Marie Schiro discussed Nancy's 1984 House committee responsibilities: "Outside of California, Nancy Pelosi is probably the least known of the key women at the Democratic National Convention." It then described her work as the chairman of the Convention '84 Host Committee, which raised $3 million to finance the convention and organized social events. Nancy led ten thousand volunteers in the efforts. As she explained to the *New York Times*, "Basically, I'm an organizer. I had five children in six years, so this is not so difficult." Schiro went to describe Nancy in her spacious living room with us five kids and my dad working on press kits, campaign buttons, and posters. She was holding a party in our house that night for the delegates from Maryland.

To secure the 1984 convention, Nancy was prepared to be a teacher. As she remembers, the world was just starting to learn about AIDS. "It was in the context of a few years earlier, several years earlier, and somebody heard of something that was going on at UCSF. There was a disease that had symptoms that had not been observed since the Middle Ages. It didn't have a name but it was something quite phenomenal and the people at UCSF, the doctors there, were recognizing that something historical was happening there. A few years later, it had a name,

AIDS, and we were trying to get the Democratic convention in San Francisco. Just imagine the way they were talking about us in the rest of the country. They want us to go there, to San Francisco where they have AIDS and all that that implies? And we said 'yes,' and really I was very proud of the decision made by the Democratic Party to come here in spite of some of the, shall we say, scare tactics and not staying by the other cities. I'm just saying by people in general, of the fright they had in coming here, it's really important to us that we could have a convention in San Francisco, California, in the beginnings, origins of HIV. In the meantime, as a concept, it was one, sometimes two, funerals a day. And in between visiting friends in hospice, or hospitals, or in their homes, we set about organizing for the convention. When people came to my house for outreach parties I'd say to a gay friend, 'Okay, let's both dip or chip in the guacamole at the same time, so they can see we are not afraid of each other.' And we got the bid and we gave people a beautiful welcome in the homes of San Franciscans."[6] Nancy's success in the effort to host the convention was her first nationally visible political activity and a harbinger of successes to come.

Proper preparation with children meant more care and feeding of the intuitive relationships. With love, leverage, and wits she managed to sense what we were thinking, what we needed, and when to push and when to withhold comment. Nancy deployed a "look" that

---

6   AIDS Memorial Quilt 25th Anniversary Reception, 2012

implied she knew what we were doing before we even planned to do it and was already helping us talk ourselves out of it. "Why would you go to that R-rated movie?" "Why would you go out late and miss curfew?" "Do you really want to make that choice?" After a certain point, Nancy knew our business so well she knew business we didn't even know we had—a skill that would come in handy counting votes in Congress.

All of this came back during the 2019 State of the Union address by Donald Trump, who was invited to address a joint session once the government had been reopened.

The speech had been postponed during the shutdown because Nancy refused to have thousands of security personnel risk their lives for a designated national security event while collecting no paychecks. The president responded by canceling her trip overseas—and the White House leaked that the trip was to visit troops in a war zone, making commercial flight into Afghanistan too unsafe for travel. A reporter asked Nancy if Trump was trying to get revenge for her taking away one of his favorite things—a primetime televised address. "I don't think the president would be that petty," Nancy said, "Do you?" We all knew that look! As Nancy Corinne told a reporter, "I knew the face." The face when we had done something wrong and she knew it and was waiting for us to 'fess up. So disappointed. "*You children wouldn't have done that*," because of course we did and now we were the ones traveling—on an Italian mother's guilt trip.

After tense negotiations, Democratic unity, rallies with furloughed workers around the country, refusal to use government money to pay for a border wall Trump had promised Mexico would fund, and near-chaos at the airports once TSA agents, air traffic controllers, flight attendants, and other aviation personnel called in sick, the shutdown was over and the president went to give the State of the Union speech.

Much was made of a few unprecedented scenes: over one hundred women members of Congress—ninety-one of them Democrats—wearing white for the suffragists and clapping when Trump said he had lowered the unemployment rate for women. The newly hired congresswomen, who had in many cases defeated his Republican cohorts, cheered in agreement.

Then there was "the clap." Another unintentionally iconic moment and generator of memes. President Trump, who has a history of aggressive tweets, asked everyone to "reject the politics of revenge, resistance and retribution and embrace the boundless potential of cooperation, compromise and the common good."

Nancy said she clapped to tell him that would be welcomed. I heard that as "welcomed" in the way it would be welcomed if we did our homework, changed the toilet paper roll, returned the car with gas, or came home by curfew—in other words, the bare minimum when she knew that we knew that we should have done more. She knows—and she knows that you know that she knows. But good try. This became a surreal moment where she seemed to be America's mom offering the wayward one encouragement with a strong and knowing side-eye of shade. The image has been replicated on tee-shirts, pins, even votive candles as once again Nancy asserted herself as the representative of a coequal branch of government, remaining calm amidst the chaos.

On her journey "from kitchen to Congress," Nancy is fiercely proud of her lessons learned as a mom of multiples—and urges parents to highlight those skills that would not otherwise show up on a résumé. She and Paul used to say the days were long but the years flew by, and they wanted to put us in the rain, shrink us, and have babies to raise all over again. They begged for grandchildren and eventually got them—in New York, Texas, Arizona, and California. They awaited each birth with the expectation of a major vote: constant check-ins to see if we were in labor, the final countdowns to delivery, the visits to the hospitals, and the bonding with each one—building their own relationships with our children, preferably without us present.

The same organizing, cajoling, quartermastering, coalition building, and encouraging that all moms do around the house is essential to the work of the House of Representatives. And none of it is possible without proper preparation. Over and over, from homework to campaigns to vote counting for the largest initiatives of our time, this adage encapsulates so much of the Nancy Pelosi way: Be ready.

The lesson: if you want to do well, prepare. Know

your why, know your strengths, know your weaknesses, know who is being honest with you and who will say yes or maybe to you, then make a subsequent promise to someone else. If you know that at 8:00 a.m. every weekday morning five children have to be fed, clothed, and sent off to school with homework, packed lunches, and bus fare, you can either execute proper preparation or expect chaos. The simple tasks multiplied by five over five days a week over years is exhausting and exhilarating, but surely as the sun rises on a school day, the tasks are necessary. The same is true in Congress: election season, transition season, budget season, and appropriations season all happen as surely as fall, winter, spring, and summer—so, like a good parent, a good legislator will prepare with anticipation, mindful of the chronology that lies ahead. Get used to synchronized chaos, treat people with equity—fairly but not the same—and let every day be a new day.

3

Be Your Own Authentic Self

THE BEST ADVICE TO GIVE anyone applying for a job, making new friends, going on a date, or running for office (which is a combination of the above) is to be yourself. Easier said than done: everyone has an opinion about what a woman leader should look like and act like. This is true even for people who have known you in your own community and see you in a supporting role as a leader but not necessarily as *the* leader.

Nancy encountered this in her first campaign for Congress. Being the state party chair means you stump for a lot of candidates. Hundreds of candidates. Suddenly when it's you as the candidate, that transition is harder. The spotlight is brighter; there's no filter; the choice is binary: yes or no, you or someone else. And that binary choice (since we do not yet have national ranked-choice voting for Congress) means that other candidates are busy putting you down. Nevertheless, at a debate Nancy was able to counter the negative campaigning with a zinger of her own: "When you came to my home all those times over the years to raise money, you praised me to the skies for my commitment to the issues; now that we are opponents, you've changed your mind. What happened?" With that, her supporters had the statement they needed to hear to know she had the toughness to fight back. The critics didn't stop then (and haven't stopped since), but Nancy stopped caring about what they thought. That gave her room to grow.

Few campaign messages were as prescient as Nancy Pelosi's 1987 congressional slogan: A Voice That Will Be Heard. At the time, she had entered the special election for Congress's 5th District of California after her friend and mentor Sala Burton died from cancer. Sala and her husband Phillip Burton and his brother John Burton were longtime San Francisco leaders who had reshaped the Democratic Party from the 1950s to the 1980s, making it more progressive and more responsive to working families. Where Sala, an elegant European immigrant whose family had left Poland just ahead of the Nazi occupation that would wipe out the population of her Jewish family's village, was genteel and diplomatic, the Burton brothers wore gruffness like armor over hearts of gold, unrelenting in their advocacy. Phillip and John were elected first to the Assembly, then to Congress, battling corporate special interests all the way. Phillip's pragmatism helped him cut deals for miners suffering from black lung disease, create Social Security disability insurance, and advance a progressive agenda even in a conservative Congress. The statue dedicated to him in the Golden Gate National Recreation Area includes an engraved paper emerging from a rumpled jacket pocket: "The way to deal with exploiters is to terrorize the bastards." Terrorize them he did, pushing votes to oppose the Vietnam War, expand the social safety net, and preserve millions of acres of natural resources—the last a tribute to his dedication to the parks as a means to give protections to native and sacred lands for the people, not to any personal love of the outdoors himself, for it was oft joked that the longest time Phil Burton spent outdoors in Yosemite was to puff down his unfiltered Chesterfield cigarettes outside Ansel Adams's "no smoking" cabin.

Phillip was a master at redistricting, could draw out districts on a cocktail napkin, and knew members' own voting and population patterns almost better than they did. He lost the race for House Majority Leader by one vote in 1976, yet remained a force with a gavel and a thundering rage for justice. His and Sala's support of Nancy Pelosi for California Democratic Party state chair in 1981 was indicative of Nancy's strengths as a leader—the endorsement card that came returned in the mail, under "I support Nancy Pelosi—Volunteer—for California Democratic Party State Chair" read "Phillip

Burton twice/Sala Burton thrice." Phillip and Nancy worked together during her term as state chair, helping win legislative seats, including his own for Congress and that of Barbara Boxer to replace John Burton, who had retired to address addiction issues. It was to be his final campaign and an inflection point in San Francisco politics: Phillip died of an aneurysm in April 1983 at age fifty-seven, just days after headlining an event held by Nancy Pelosi to attract the 1984 Democratic National Convention to their hometown. San Francisco won the bid, and Nancy would lead the host committee. But first she would help elect her friend Sala Burton to Congress.

Sala's race was born of sadness: in shock over her husband's death and determined to carry forth his legacy, she ran to champion jobs, peace, health care, and the environment. She encountered sexism from the start, as male politicians actually said out loud to the press that Phil had asked them to "take care of Sala." Sala took care of herself. A founder of the Democratic Study Group, longtime advocate for Soviet Jewry, and ambassador for her husband's political agenda, she was a forceful and nurturing talent in her own right. And as a teenage volunteer on her campaigns and intern in her office, I saw firsthand that Sala knew the power of ideas, the importance of representation, and the strength of immigrants. When she announced in January 1987 that she would be retiring from Congress due to cancer, several prominent San Francisco politicians, including some who had claimed Phil had asked them to "take care of Sala" four years before, were publicly declaring their intentions. But Sala had other plans: calling Nancy, John, and other close friends to her bedside, she asked Nancy Pelosi to run for her seat in the 1988 election. Sala felt that Nancy would be effective because she knew the issues, had amassed a grassroots army of ten thousand volunteers to help with the 1984 Democratic National Convention, and had helped win the United States Senate in 1986 as finance chair of the Democratic Senatorial Campaign Committee. Sala theorized that the chairmen—Biden, Kennedy, Hollings—would help San Francisco and the representative who'd helped them win their gavels. We had a family meeting, and we urged Nancy to run. "You love the issues, you should run and you will win," Paul Pelosi told his wife, "but you should do it because you want to, not because people are asking you." We children agreed, but it came down to a conversation with my sister Alexandra, then a junior in high school. The pitch: "Mommy has this opportunity, but it would start the summer before your senior year of high school, so it's up to you. I would be gone three days a week but home on the weekends." Alexandra, who like most teenagers didn't sweat the prospect of losing the close supervision of an eagle-eyed mom three days a week, gave her blessing in the high school vernacular of the times: "Mother. Get a life."

Only a few days following the bedside endorsement, Sala died. And Nancy went to get a[nother] life.

Nancy entered the campaign with a heavy heart,

four incumbent San Francisco supervisors in the race, and a campaign plan that was six thousand votes short. At the very first campaign meeting, there was a series of butcher paper sheets posted around the campaign office with the expected vote tallies from each neighborhood from Bayview Hunter's Point to the Sunset District. But there was no TOTALS sheet, and Nancy quickly glanced around the room, mentally calculated the totals, and said, "You said I need 35,000 people out of 100,000 voters—but these only add up to 29,000." That set the tone of the campaign: Nancy may have been a first-time candidate, but she was not a first-time campaigner. So the first task was to get another six thousand votes. And the second was to get to know every one of those 35,000 voters as intimately as a seven-week campaign would allow.

Sala and John Burton had endorsed Nancy, as had Congresswoman Geraldine Ferraro, the first woman nominated for vice president by a major political party, and longtime friend Lt. Governor Leo McCarthy. Most of the city service unions as well as the then self-described gay and lesbian (now LGBTQ) community was for Harry Britt, with a few hundred notable exceptions led by campaign cochair James Hormel, who would go on to be the nation's first openly gay ambassador under President Clinton; Scott Douglass, who had driven Jimmy Carter's one-car caravan from the New Hampshire campaign to the Carter White House; and the *Bay Times* editor, Kim Corsaro. Assembly speaker Willie Brown split his endorsement between Nancy and supervisor Doris Ward, and the Democratic Party Clubs were all over the map, so the race for endorsements and volunteers was fierce.

Like all campaigns that combine a small start-up with a large social movement, there were intense moments. The kickoff at the Longshoremen's Hall with campaign cochairs Jimmy Herman and LeRoy King was packed with people. But they needed to be organized. Enter AFSCME, the Association of Federal, State, County, and Municipal Employees, who were among Nancy's first and strongest supporters, and the farmworkers with their lead organizers: Fred Ross Sr. and Fred Ross Jr. Fred Ross Sr. had been an organizer of the legendary Community Service Organization, cofounded by the Burtons' longtime friend and congressional colleague Eddie Roybal-Allard from Los Angeles, whose daughter Lucille succeeded him in Congress and is a member of the Congressional Hispanic Caucus her father cofounded and wields a gavel as an Appropriations Subcommittee Chair. Fred had organized with Cesar Chavez and Dolores Huerta, cofounders of the Farm Workers Association, and trained a generation of organizers.

With Fred Ross Sr. directing volunteers to cold-call the phone book to harness our persuasion skills and Fred Ross Jr. and Marshall Ganz organizing over a hundred house meetings in key communities to identify and turn out those 35,000 (not 29,000) votes, the Pelosi for Congress campaign was focused on taking the campaign to the community. From the couple dozen friends future Supervisor Leslie Katz assembled in her apartment to one hundred people at the Saint Patrick's Day party packing the home of Sharon Allen (a daughter of Leo T. McCarthy) to the hundreds of people dancing at the Oasis nightclub, where Cynthia Smith (now Birmingham) convinced the hosts to put Pelosi for Congress pins in the disco's goodie bowls, every house meeting had a singular goal: build people power to get Nancy to the House, one house party at a time. The house meeting model was used by Martin Luther King Jr. in the 1950s and 1960s, by the Farm Workers in the 1960s and 1970s, and by Neighbor to Neighbor, organizers for peace in Central America, in the 1980s.

In the early days of her house meetings, Nancy's "rap" (speech) was always the same—her personal story as a Democratic volunteer, dedicated wife and mother, advocate for AIDS patients, jobs, and justice followed by "the ask" for help—but her delivery improved over the weeks. A naturally shy person, Nancy was much more comfortable talking about being a vote in Congress to fight the AIDS epidemic that was ravaging San Francisco, push for jobs, or end Contra Aid (money the Reagan Administration was paying to arm the "Contra" rebels against the Nicaraguan government) than she was about extolling her own virtues. It would be years into her service in Congress before she would brag about her legislative skills. Ever aware of the gender stereotypes, she would speak directly about her role as a mother and kitchen quartermaster.

And even though we were aged sixteen to twenty-two,

with all but Alexandra in college, people still asked her, "Who's going to take care of your children?" Nancy knew better than to dismiss or bristle at the question, choosing to respond with the spirit that voters wanted to know she was going to make the job her top priority and that women voters were asking her what they were being asked themselves in their professional endeavors. So Nancy would smile and say, "Raising my children forged me; being a mother is my greatest joy; now four of them are in college, and Alexandra is very close with her father. They know that I will work hard to represent San Francisco and support my campaign."

Because Nancy had been a hands-on mom, many of her grassroots volunteers knew her from her days driving carpools in her Jeep Wagoneer, chaperoning field trips, baking cupcakes, and volunteering in the libraries before, during, and after being a library commissioner. They didn't know her views on all the issues, but they knew her as a person, and "I trusted her with my kids" was a strong signal to people that Nancy was an authentic person who immersed herself in her children's lives and was dependable. Others were recruited among the ten thousand convention volunteers who had worked side by side with Nancy slicing vegetables for an outreach party or stuffing the delegate packets into denim briefcases. That support was critical in winning: on election night one proud organizer of a "perfect precinct"—wherein 100 percent of the identified Pelosi voters turned out at the polls—was a woman who worked at the Convent of the Sacred Heart school, which we four Pelosi girls had attended for most of the 1970s and 1980s (a cumulative total of forty-eight years between us). They knew the authentic Nancy as a mom and as a volunteer—and they trusted her.

Most people have never met their representative or a candidate for Congress, so to go into the community where they can come ask questions and define the kind of leadership they want is critical to forming a close bond. Picture 120 job interviews with two thousand people in seven weeks and you get the idea. Each meeting is different, but the discipline of sharing her personal story, explaining her vision for the future, detailing her plan to win, and attracting support with specific commitments and then following through was the same pattern for all.

Those early weeks of campaigning not only made Nancy a contender but also set the indefatigable pace she has been on ever since, always moving with the click-clack of her heels on marble or pavement from one meeting to the next, each a new experience given its own unique attention and focus on detail. To this day Nancy will tell candidates to recruit their grassroots army in the neighborhoods: hold one hundred house parties and recruit one thousand volunteers so that you know the grassroots down to every blade of grass, and you can cultivate leadership and relationships. No matter how far you might advance in public service, each day has to have that grassroots component and openness to other people and their ideas.

BE YOUR OWN AUTHENTIC SELF

Oftentimes the toughest critics come from your own ethnic community: they want to know that you know who you are and never forget where you come from. They want to see you respect their traditions and walk humbly as their representative. Once you can win your community over, they will be behind you all the way. Raised on the spaghetti suppers, cakewalks, and social events at St. Leo's Catholic Church Parish in Baltimore, Nancy knew how to make the rounds in the Italian Catholic communities of San Francisco. She went to the churches, the pasta feeds, and the bingo games, not to campaign during the games—because no smart person wants to come between the Italian ladies and their multiple bingo cards—but to "pay my respects and sweeten the pot." And she had a secret weapon no consultant could pay for: the grassroots army led by the Nana Brigade.

The original Nana was her mother-in-law, Corinne Pelosi, née Bianchi, who lived in San Francisco and had deep roots in the community. After coming to America from Italy through Ellis Island a few years after Nancy's mother Annunciata had, Corinne was raised in California and married her husband John, who had emigrated from Italy through Peru, and together they raised their boys in the Marina District of San Francisco. Their eldest, Ronald, had served as a county supervisor, and the family was active in civic affairs and their parish of St. Vincent de Paul. During the winter and spring of 1987, the Nana Brigade sat around the dining room table, where generations of Pelosis had been raised, and pored over precinct reports of every Italian surname from the voter file. While arguing a bit over what part of Italy the voters with certain surnames were from and taking care not to stain the glass that covered the lace that covered the wood tabletop, they inked handwritten postcards urging every Italian American voter they could find to cast a ballot for Corinne's daughter-in-law.

From the support of the Burtons to the Italian community to the school networks to organized labor—the UFW farmworkers, AFSCME public service workers, ILWU dockworkers, public school teachers, and nurses— Nancy had the makings of a base that was loyal to her as a person, and on top of that she built the structure one house meeting, one community event, one principled fight at a time. One hundred and twenty house meetings and innumerable phone banks and precinct walks later, Nancy was within striking distance.

That ability to build a movement around people with a common purpose—to win an election and achieve a specific kind of official representation—with care, ever present in the moment, attendant to every detail, and observant of those around her was Nancy's coming into her own authentic self. Her brother Tommy D'Alesandro III, who had followed their father into politics and served a term as mayor, came out to check on his little sister and gave the ultimate seal of approval: "She's organizing the grassroots like we do campaigns in Baltimore." Indeed, the foot soldier in her mother's moccasin army had fused her Baltimore background and San Francisco life into her own identity, giving her a network that she still calls "the ever-widening circle of friends." To this day, house meeting hosts from 1987 sign Nancy's nomination papers, work the phone banks, and participate in her quarterly "politics and eggs" grassroots breakfasts.

Eleven days before the election, a poll came out that put the race within the 4 percent margin of error in a field presuming 100,000 total votes. Our collective hearts sank. This was a key test of mettle: just when we thought we had all the voters we needed and had done the work to turn from identification to persuasion to mobilization, we had to go back to those same doors where people had said no or maybe and identify four thousand more yes votes, persuade and mobilize them to widen that circle of friends. Moment of truth: Nancy looked through the charts on the walls and quizzed each area coordinator down to the household to see where she could earn extra votes. Back into the field we went with the house meeting hosts turned neighborhood precinct captains, phone bankers, and Nana Brigade now calling to follow up on their postcards. The extra push worked. On April 7, 1987, Nancy won with 38,021 votes to her top opponent Harry Britt's 34,031 votes. (Although the raw numbers turned out to be extra because she would have won with 35,000, pushing for more with a sense of urgency lifted up the entire effort. Had we only targeted the 35,000 voters she needed, not the 39,000 voters she ultimately identified, the victory might not have been assured.) Lesson in vote counting: always add more to your target, because there is safety in numbers.

The primary election was tantamount to winning a general election in highly Democratic San Francisco, so between April 7 and June 2 Nancy set out to win the campaign by unifying the Democratic voters around her and preparing for the 1988 election. She deployed her teams to areas where she had won, starting with her strongholds in Chinatown, to remind people to vote in the runoff—and to areas she had not, campaigning in the Castro District and eventually appearing with Britt at June Pride events. She met with the groups who had endorsed her opponents. In a story that Nancy tells every year at the AFSCME PEOPLE Congressional Candidates Boot Camp, John Burton joked that the unions who did not support Nancy could "call AFSCME" to make an appointment—but in truth she was gracious in victory and ready to work with everyone. The enthusiasms and disappointments were as intense at the end as they were from the start. Being a good winner helped Nancy assume the job with a good impression that she would represent everyone—not just her voters—establish more open lines of communication in the LGBTQ community to fully engage with the fight against the AIDS epidemic, be ready to work with the four county supervisors—Britt, Ward, Maher, and Silver—who were going back to City Hall, and prepare to be "a voice that will be heard."

Nancy Pelosi was the unexpected candidate. She was

not groomed to run, she was not expected to run, she had turned down other requests from party leaders to run. Yet when she did run, she was ready because she was her own authentic self. People attacked her for "only being a mom"—one female columnist said Nancy couldn't "hold the clipboard" of a supervisor on the issues—as if stay-at-home moms don't read the paper or help with homework or engage in children's education and learn new things (and Nancy was prepared for the sad reality that women will go after other women by using sexist tropes like "moms don't know issues"). Another candidate had called her a dilettante for being a party leader, even though as party leader she raised the money needed to register one million voters in the 1982 election and drafted a platform and campaign messaging that won elections. She was attacked for having a wealthy husband and a big home by the very people who had spent countless hours in our family home as we five kids passed appetizers to the guests attending her Volunteers In Politics (VIP) program, where if you paid a dollar a month you got a party newsletter (zip sorted in that living room by us) and invitations to come hear from party leaders and civic advocates from Phil Burton and Alan Cranston to Cesar Chavez and Dolores Huerta. She was attacked for raising money from a national base—although that national base of voters had funded the 1984 Democratic National Convention in San Francisco when she served as host committee chair and the successful 1986 Democratic effort to win back the United States Senate when she worked as finance director for the Democratic Senatorial Campaign Committee. And she was attacked for receiving "Sala Burton's deathbed endorsement"—a rather ghoulish way for people to attack the endorsement of a congresswoman endorsing a woman as her successor—but the truth was every time people said that it cemented Nancy's support from Burton voters.

Each of those attacks was designed to undermine her—sometimes in sexist ways by women. They tried it all! I can remember going into coffee shops and hearing people debate these very issues. It's surreal when it's the first time you hear them talking about your parent or when you drive through town and see their signs defaced or when you get yelled at (once literally spat at) by really angry supporters of your parent's opponent who expect you to keep your cool lest you lose votes for them. But Nancy anticipated that too—and told us all that she knew who she was and what she cared about, had a vision and a plan that attracted over 1,500 volunteers to our movement, and was willing to withstand any slings and arrows that came her way. And she insisted that her campaign remain positive, stay focused, and build bridges. It worked.

Being your own authentic self was not only a constant theme we saw from Nancy during her cross-country travels in the critical 2018 election cycle. It was the number-one piece of advice she gave (and continues to give) to leaders of all backgrounds—whether to grassroots organizations from a certain state, a candidate's group of strong supporters, or a crowd of young, passionate, and aspiring women leaders.

The lesson: Be your own authentic self, not someone else's idea of what you are, and prepare to share who you are with an open heart. You don't want to be anybody else—you want to be you. The most authentic, sincere presentation of you is you. You may have mentors, you may have role models, and that's a good thing, but know you own power and give yourself credit for what you bring to it. What is your purpose? What is your call to service? What is your North Star? Know about it. Show your vision. People want to respect your judgment. You will not know everything on every subject, but you need knowledge and strategic judgment about your main pull into service. What is your plan? How do you plan to persuade other people toward your vision or how do you plan to join them as you build coalitions? And then—the connection. You can have all the vision and knowledge and strategic thinking in the world, but you must connect with people. And once you connect, stick with your vision, adjust your plan, and widen your circle of friends and family to respond to attacks. Nancy's was a unique candidacy for Congress and for Speaker, but the litany of attacks is all too typical. Anticipate these attacks and be ready with a response that your supporters can echo. You cannot shy away from engaging: a direct attack requires a direct response from you. Defend yourself while keeping friendship in your voice, because people may not be assuming the worst about you but rather simply repeating what they heard from someone else and are open for more information. That may not win over every voter— at least not right away—but you can't expect to avoid the personal attacks or ignore them. People don't expect you to agree with them on every issue, or to approve of everything you've done, in order to support you. Do what shy, never-going-to-run Nancy Pelosi did when she ran: give the voters a chance to see your heart if you want them to trust you with theirs, and get ready to fight for them if you want them to fight for you. Know what you believe. Know about what you believe. Have a plan to act upon your values and make a difference. If you go talk about that people will be drawn to you—because they will know that you know who you are.

4

Claim Your Seat at the Table

NANCY HAS SAID FOR YEARS, "Nothing is more whole-some to politics than the increased participation of women." Under her leadership, women are not only wel-comed with a seat at the table—but with a seat at the head of the table, wielding a gavel.

Long before she entered Congress, Nancy had an experience of getting a seat at the table that foretold major events in American history.

The year was 1958. The setting was the United Nations Association of Maryland dinner in Baltimore. Mayor D'Alesandro and his wife were expected to attend. The First Lady was sick, so her daughter Nancy went in her stead. As a member of the United Nations

Association of High School Students, Nancy was offered a seat with her cohorts. But she chose to sit at her father's table with the guest speaker—Senator John F. Kennedy of Massachusetts.

Ever gracious, Nancy gently turned down the invitation from the High School Association to sit at their table. She said to them, "I'd be so honored, but I'm taking my mother's place tonight, and I couldn't possibly leave this empty seat."

In a moment memorialized by a photograph that would ricochet through history, the mayor's daughter met the Massachusetts senator. Though many people predicted that John F. Kennedy would go on to be elected president of the United States, absolutely no one could have predicted that Nancy D'Alesandro would go on to be elected the first and second woman speaker of the House. Or that Nancy Pelosi would be awarded the John F. Kennedy Profiles in Courage Award "for putting the national interest above her party's interest to expand access to health care for all Americans and then, against a wave of political attacks, leading the effort to retake the majority and elect the most diverse Congress in our nation's history."[7]

The dinner table was significant for another reason: as a member of the High School United Nations Association, Nancy was an avid reader of history and proponent of

7   John F. Kennedy Profile in Courage Award 2019, https://www.jfklibrary .org/events-and-awards/profile-in-courage-award/award-recipients/nancy -pelosi-2019.

building American "soft power" in the diplomatic realm. The nuns at her school, the Institute of Notre Dame, have a framed statement in the school vestibule that reads "School is not a Prison, it is not a Playground, it is Time, it is Opportunity." Nancy took that discipline to heart, learning academics and planning to leave Baltimore for Washington, DC.

With some lobbying, Nancy convinced her parents to let her attend Trinity College (now University) in Washington, DC, and major in political science. The Trinity nuns' theory of learning was expressed by quoting the English historian J. R. Seeley: "History without political science has no fruit; political science with no history has no root." Those studies and a book she had read, *Cry, the Beloved Country* by South African writer Alan Paton, called Nancy to a summer school class at Georgetown University studying Africa South of the Sahara taught by the legendary professor Dr. Carroll Quigley and attended by her future husband, Paul Pelosi. A native of San Francisco, Paul was the president of the Georgetown School of Foreign Service student body and friends with the brother of Nancy's college roommate. One thing led to another, and the couple was married a few years later. Nearly sixty years later, Nancy and Paul have been married fifty-six years and remain close to their college roommates and friends, getting together at least twice year as a group and connecting constantly.

Rarely does one moment at the table imprint itself on a personal and political journey—but Nancy's did.

And the lesson for young people—especially young women—is this: take your seat at the table. Be confident in your ability to be there; to be present; to make a difference—and if you can't make a difference, make an impression—and bring other people with you. Most of all, she says, "be ready."

This was true in 1973 as Nancy got a call from then San Francisco mayor Joe Alioto. She recalls the conversation as follows:

"Nancy, this is Joe Alioto, this is the Mayor. What are you doing? Making a great big pot of pasta fagioli?"

"No, Mr. Mayor, I'm reading the newspaper," she replied.

"I want to appoint you to the library commission."

At first, Nancy declined. "I love the library, but I'll just be a volunteer. Why don't you give the title to somebody else, because I know it's a very coveted position?" And Alioto responded: "No, no, no; don't tell me that. One day you may want to run for office, and being a library commissioner is a good credential." Although Nancy insisted that she was "absolutely never, never running for office," she agreed to serve on the library commission. Days later, surrounded by five children aged three to nine crawling in and under the mayor's desk, Nancy took her seat at the table—and loved it. She got to know people, they cared about her opinion, and they did great work like taking their hearings out into the community to the branch libraries and seeing firsthand what the people needed.

The lesson: don't deny yourself a seat at the table. If there is an opportunity to get credit for your work and become a leader in your field, take it. Too often women do what Nancy did initially: offer to continue in uncredited volunteer work while the men are already clamoring for the position, whether or not they ever stepped foot in a library. Women tend to second- or third-guess ourselves, but the reason Nancy tells this origin story is to teach us to shake off doubts, respond to what others see in us, and claim that seat at the table. As Nancy's Baltimore nuns said about school—it is Time, it is Opportunity.

Once again, taking her seat at the table was an inflection point: experience, community, and connections. As it happened, the local libraries needed state funding, so she started to get to know her assembly member, Leo McCarthy. One thing led to another, and Nancy met Governor Jerry Brown. Had she remained a volunteer and not taken the library commissioner position, where her vote mattered and her opinion and work could help make a difference at scale, Nancy might not have advanced in party politics. But with a little prodding, she was ready to serve as a commissioner and enjoyed doing the work of the San Francisco Library with the added responsibility of helping to set its course.

Having met Jerry Brown and seen the excitement around his 1976 candidacy for president against

frontrunner Jimmy Carter of Georgia, Nancy called
Leo McCarthy, then serving as Brown's campaign chair,
and encouraged them to run in the Maryland primary.
She introduced this young dynamic candidate to the
D'Alesandro operation—her parents and her brother,
"Young Tommy, " former Baltimore mayor and friend
of San Francisco Mayor Alioto. It was quite a culture
shock—California casual meets Baltimore New Deal
Democrats—never more so than when Jerry Brown
addressed a campus full of young people practically
hanging from the rafters and urged them all to go home
and . . . ("get out the vote!" Tommy D'Alesandro III
thought to himself) "put a brick in your toilet [tank]!"
Brown exhorted. The crowd cheered. Not what they'd
expected, but the D'Alesandros got to work and to *nearly*
everyone's surprise but theirs, Jerry Brown won the
Maryland primary and credited Nancy Pelosi as the archi-
tect of his victory. He named her as a delegate to the convention and later as a representative on the Democratic
National Committee. Within a few months, Jimmy
Carter had won the presidency, and Nancy Pelosi was
the Northern Chair of the California Democratic Party.
She thought both of them had reached their respective
political heights. But history had another plan—more
opportunities and more tables of power for Nancy to be
a "first."

Too often, Nancy has said, when a woman achieves a
seat at the table, people try to instill doubt that a woman
can do a certain job when she's "the first," whether it's

the first woman to head a major corporation or the first woman Army general. She considered her election as the first woman party leader as a challenge to remove all doubt in anyone's mind that women can do any job in America. There will always be people projecting doubt or "leadership tests" on women and people of color and LGBTQ Americans that they don't think to impose on white men. When a woman wants to lead, it's "Who said she could run?" or "Give us a list." When she runs, it's "in the biggest test of her leadership/speakership/chairwomanship to date." When she delivers, it's "We did that."

That is, if the women get to speak at all. Sometimes men simply talk over the women, implying that they should be lucky just to be there at the table—no need to talk.

Never was that more true than at the dinner table during Nancy's early years in Congress. On Tuesday nights she would often have dinner with a close group of mostly male colleagues and 25 percent of the House Democratic Women's Caucus—that is to say, three out of only twelve Democratic congresswomen: Barbara Boxer of California and Barbara Kennelly of Connecticut. The breaking point for the three women came one night as the congressmen were sitting around the table discussing the births of their children. "Surely now they will ask us mothers what we think," whispered the congresswomen, who had nine children among them. No. Alas—not even childbirth was a topic the men deemed worthy to have input from the women.

There was a real conspiracy of silence. Women were

basically not telling their stories. The attitude was, "Look, you're lucky to just be here in the room. Don't blow it for everybody else by being so female." But Nancy, Barbara, and Barbara wanted to tell their stories and lift up other people's stories. There is a tremendous amount of courage that women have when they talk about their own experiences with regard to their choices. That may not seem as important now in this era of storytelling and the public confessional, but it was a very different time thirty years ago. Women needed to help each other feel so confident at the table of power that they felt welcome not only to speak up but to bring other women with them. The prospect of having a sisterhood, of seeing women lead together with strength, not competition or chauvinism, was inspiring.

So Nancy and her cohorts made a decision: let's elect more women. She, Boxer, and Kennelly were three of twelve Democratic congresswomen; there were eleven Republican congresswomen. Over the years, with a conscious decision to recruit and fund and elect women, the numbers swelled to 106 women in 2019: ninety-one Democrats and fifteen Republicans. "Having more women in Congress is a decision," Nancy always says. "Because we made a decision that every year we would increase the number. We would say 'Get out there, run, do what you can do. We can help.'"

The creation and growth of women's advocacy and training networks also gave more candidates the ability to meet donors, recruit grassroots supporters, and appeal to women trailblazers in business and in government. The year 1992 was the so-called Year of the Woman— five female senators were elected and twenty-four more women got elected to Congress, including Nancy's long- time friend and sister in service, Representative Anna Eshoo, who won with a promise to "challenge the sacred cows" and went on to become a national leader in tech- nology and health care and spearhead the innovation agenda to bring STEAM into education and employment for women and girls. Now the moms might well be asked for their input on childbirth—but they were not coming to discuss "women's issues" unless those issues included climate, national security, diplomacy, economics, health care, civil rights, and the future of jobs, technology, and work.

Years later, in her first days as the House Democratic leader, Nancy Pelosi had another portentous "seat at the table" moment. This time, it was at the White House. It was 2003, and although Nancy had been to the White House many times, this meeting felt different.

This is how Nancy describes her first meeting with then-President George W. Bush as elected leader of the Democrats in Congress: "I had no apprehension about going to this meeting. Still, I felt different. I walked into the room, and then as I went into the room and the door closed behind me, in this small room at a small table with those people, I realized this was unlike any other meeting I'd ever been to in the White House. In fact, it was unlike any meeting that any woman had ever been to at the

White House. I was there, not with derivative power as an appointee or staff person of the president. I was there elected by the Democrats in the Congress of the United States to represent a coequal branch of government. As President Bush graciously welcomed me to the meeting, I was feeling really closed-in in my chair. I mean, I've never had that sensation before or since. I was really crowded on my chair. And there was Susan B. Anthony, Lucretia Mott, Elizabeth Cady Stanton, Sojourner Truth, Alice Paul. They were all on the chair—you name more—they were all on the chair. And I could hear them say: 'At last, we have a seat at the table.' And then they were gone. And my first thought was, we want more: more women, more diversity, more power."

Sharing that experience with audiences across the country, in candidate recruitment, and in House committee assignments, Nancy did the specific and intentional work to make sure that we would have more women in power and therefore more authentic policy conversations about the priorities and lived experiences of the American people.

Year later, as the economy was crashing in 2008, Nancy found herself at the table in the White House at a daunting series of meetings on which the entire economy depended. Well able to breathe the air at that altitude, she was going to need all her strength to deal with the panic of those who were gasping. As Speaker of the House, Nancy had worked with President George W. Bush despite their extreme differences on his war in Iraq.

They passed on a fiscal stimulus bill and a large energy bill that raised fuel efficiency standards, taking the equivalent of millions of cars off the roads. But nothing had prepared anyone for what happened in the fall of 2008 when the global economy risked collapse—and the Bush administration almost didn't tell Congress about it.

As Nancy told the story, she was in her office discussing the latest financial news and mentioned that she had not received her usual briefing from Treasury Secretary Hank Paulson. In that time, Lehman Bros. had filed for bankruptcy, Merrill Lynch had faced failure and had been purchased by Bank of America, and AIG had survived only after a Federal Reserve bailout. After the meeting at 3 p.m., she called Secretary Paulson and asked him to come the next morning to brief the leadership: "Then came his stunning response: 'Madam Speaker, tomorrow morning will be too late.'"[8]

Faced with that shocking news, Nancy had a choice: let the president take the blame he was "saving" for his successor who would be elected ten weeks later, or act decisively for the good of the country and the economy. She chose the latter.

Congresswoman Eshoo, who had been waiting to catch up with Nancy that afternoon, remembers the scene: "Everyone was panicked but not Nancy. She knew what to do. She said, 'They are giving me a prescription of what they want—but I'm going to write my own bill.'"

At a White House meeting to negotiate the terms and

---

8   Nancy Pelosi, *USA Today*, September 17, 2013.

protections of a $700 million bailout, House Republicans who had resisted regulation, discipline, and supervision now opposed government intervention. Democrats had gone to the White House expecting to come out with a deal to help Main Street and Wall Street, but the Republicans refused to do more than bail out the banks, proffering no assistance to American families whose savings and investments were wiped out. As the Democrats regrouped in the Roosevelt Room, Treasury Secretary Hank Paulson burst in. Paulson literally dropped to one knee in front of Nancy and begged her: "Don't blow this thing up." Nancy had been working with the president, and Bush had said as much in the meeting. She was steady in response: "Hank, I didn't know you were Catholic." She added, "It's not me blowing this up, it's the Republicans." Paulson sighed. "I know," he said. (Those in the room later said he was joking.)

There was no appetite for bailing out big banks, yet the economy had to be saved. Nancy promised that House Democrats would produce 120 votes (218 were needed for a House majority), while Republicans pledged 100 votes. When the vote came up the first time, Democrats put forward 140 votes, but just 65 Republicans supported President Bush's approach. The bill failed. And as it went down, so did the stock market. The Dow dropped 778 points, the single largest one-day drop in its history. George Miller remembers: "She told the Caucus we have to do this for the country. We delivered our votes, but Republicans killed the bill on the first vote and the market crashed. That was the validation of how serious this was. Then the vote was done. Her credibility went up—to save the nation was more important than to suffer the political consequences of taking a tough vote. Days later the bill returned to the floor, the Republicans brought their votes this time, and the bill passed."

The lesson here is to have courage when you come to the table. Nancy often says, "It's so important for women to have the confidence, to have the courage to go out there and just jump into the arena. When you are there, remember the responsibility to represent the people. It is not about getting to the table but working with purpose once you are there."

In addition, "Recognize your responsibility to encourage other people who are on their own paths to public service. It is amazing how much you can accomplish if you are willing to share the credit."

Or in Speaker Pelosi's case, share the gavels. In the 116th Congress, nine House committees are convened by women: committee chairwomen include Nita Lowey (appropriations), Maxine Waters (financial services), Eddie Bernice Johnson (science, space, and technology), Zoe Lofgren (House administration), Nydia Velázquez (small business), Carolyn Maloney (joint economic committee), and Kathy Castor (select committee on the climate crisis). Thirty-six subcommittee gavels are held by women, including a record nine freshman congresswomen. By contrast, when the "Watergate Babies" were elected in a 1974 post-Nixon sweep, not a single freshman got a gavel; but under Speaker Pelosi, eighteen of the 2018 Majority Makers have gavels, eight chairmen and ten chairwomen. That is what making a decision to include women at the table—and at the head of the table—looks like. And as always, Nancy Pelosi wants more. Having women in power means celebrating women in power.

Nancy has made a conscious effort to add statues of women to the Capitol—lasting monuments to activists including Rosa Parks and Sojourner Truth. At the ceremony with First Lady Michelle Obama and eight of Truth's relatives in attendance, Nancy said:

> In Sojourner Truth's lifelong fight for equality, she fought to end slavery, to expand opportunity, and she saw the end of a civil war that had torn apart our country. As the first woman Speaker of the House, I am particularly grateful for Sojourner's work for women's suffrage. As she bravely said, "I am glad to see that men are getting their rights, but I want women to get theirs, and while the water is stirring, I will step into the pool."

Michelle Obama said, "And just as Susan B. Anthony, Elizabeth Cady Stanton, Lucretia Mott would be pleased to know that we have a woman serving as the Speaker of the House of Representatives, I hope that Sojourner Truth would be proud to see me, a descendant of slaves, serving as the First Lady of the United States of America. We are all here because, as my husband says time and time again, we stand on the shoulders of giants like Sojourner Truth."

The lesson: step into the pool; step up to the table; enter with confidence knowing that you belong; and bring others with you. Say yes, because you are being asked by someone who sees something in you. It may be something they need—like representation or a friendly vote or a plan to make complicated choices to address a crisis—but seize the opportunity and be confident enough in your skills and talent assessments to bring others with you.

As Nancy says:

With all the respect in the world for what my male colleagues bring to the table, this is where I say to women candidates all the time, "We need you to run. We need that diversity of opinion." When I became House Democratic Leader, people would say to me, after a meeting, "Do you know how different that meeting would have been if a man were conducting it?" Because I do think that women have a consensus-building attitude of listening and prioritizing working together collaboratively, maybe more than people are used to. I'm not saying men don't do it, but I'm saying women maybe do it more. And so what I say to women is, "It's not that women are better than men, it just means you cannot have a conversation about the future of the country without half the population at the table. We want the people at the table to reflect America. As our numbers grew our power grew, then our policies grew as well. When young women see you are at the table, it gives confidence that their voices are at the table."

5

Build Strategic Alliances

NANCY TRACES HER FIRST STRATEGIC alliance to age seven. Her father was elected Baltimore mayor, and the family was at City Hall. The family rule was, "Don't talk to strangers." A stranger entered and asked Nancy and her brother Joey if they were excited for their dad. Nancy did not respond. It turns out that the "stranger" was the outgoing mayor, Theodore Roosevelt McKeldin. Joey said he would tell Mommy that Nancy wasn't polite to the mayor. Nancy told Joey that she would tell Mommy he had spoken to a stranger. They made a no-squealing rule, and her first strategic alliance was formed.

To this day she does not condone squealing, especially because being the leader means being the keeper of

many secrets. But before there are confidences, there are
more fundamental questions that as party leader, whip,
and Speaker, Nancy Pelosi has to ask: "do they want to
be led?" Then you can decide if they want to be led by
you or your cohort. Many a Democratic Party group is
a raucous caucus of opinionated people, each wanting to
press forward with their own vision and plan. Some are
better than others in working in communities and coalitions—and one way to gauge their aptitude is to make
an honest assessment of who wants to organize together,
who wants to counter-organize, and who did not realize
before they ran for a legislative position that they were
running to join other members in a deliberative body
where the majority vote is the coin of the realm. But we
all soon find out.

And so the advice Nancy Pelosi has offered over the
years to build strategic alliances is to begin with a personal assessment: Do they want to be alone or in teams?
Are they willing to put egos and personalities aside to
pursue a common goal? Then you can decide who should
lead them and figure out where one person will join in
coalition where people lead each other depending on the
issue and the cause. If the person running doesn't work
with other people, says they like to take long walks on
the beach alone, works in a homogenous environment, or
actively runs against the party, they are less likely to want
to be led than the people who worked in community,
played team sports, succeeded in other legislatures or city

councils or nonprofit boards, and want to lead with consensus and so have more incentive to build it.

Most of that assessment will vary from issue to issue in what Nancy calls the "kaleidoscope" of politics. For example, when it comes to the environment, some of the same evangelicals and secular humanists who oppose each other with respect to the separation of church and state agree on the urgent need to face the climate crisis and share a conservationist agenda to preserve natural resources. You never know where you might find common cause with people, but when you learn how they organize and interact with people, you get a better sense of the things they care about, how they work together in community, and what ambassadors can bring them together for days or even years of shuttle diplomacy to bridge the political polarization and personality differences. Progress is possible.

As the kaleidoscope shifts and today's allies are tomorrow's adversaries, Nancy Pelosi often quotes her late friend, Congresswoman Lindy Boggs: "Never fight each fight as if it were your last," because you will need each other again. Easier said than done—which is why strategic alliances require a desire to do something together and a desire to be led, if not by another person then at least by a commitment to personal and political discipline. They also require a sense of purpose. If all people do is attack you, they are making a decision that they'd rather lead themselves and you should never count on them. You may happen to agree on something, but don't count on them helping you or giving you support. Nancy is quite clear about reading people and understanding that while all activists are by nature dissatisfied—and should be—some want to be part of a process and some want to remain completely independent. That's okay. Just know what you want and can expect.

There are tremendous advocates for the causes we love who prefer to be "nonpolitical" because they feel their effectiveness is best communicated in a nonpartisan space. It is still a vital strategic alliance. For example, ever since she became leader seventeen years ago, Nancy has convened Veterans Services Organizations roundtables to bring stakeholders together with the relevant committees of jurisdiction in Congress, including armed services, appropriations, budget, and veterans affairs. Over the years, these meetings have become a regular part of the Democratic caucuses' bipartisan work to meet the needs of America's veterans, military families, and caregivers. Giving her their "Unsung Hero" award in 2004, the American Legion recognized her efforts to "leave no veteran behind" and allow new ones to find their voices, strengthening strategic alliances. This might have been unexpected to some that the liberal leader would be at the center of traditionally conservative military communities, but Nancy found her calling due in part to her brothers' and nephew's service in the military and her commitment to separate her opposition to the Iraq War from her care and concern for the warriors and their families.

Political strategic alliances depend on inside-outside mobilization. As Nancy often says: Congress has to do the legislative work of *inside* maneuvering, but the *outside mobilization* is what makes all the difference. Nancy's longtime friend, the late Father Floyd Lotito of St. Anthony's Dining Room, with whom she served the venerable soup kitchen's 35 millionth meal, once missed a meeting in Representative Pelosi's congressional district office. When they called to find out where he was, staff learned he was indeed on site—at a hunger strike outside, gently demonstrating what the plight of his flock would be without the federal funds to feed them. Rather than go to her office to tell her, Father Floyd stayed outside her building to show the media. Inside one day, outside the next, all in a spirit of remembering the friendship and inside-outside mobilization. That is the nature of activists who speak truth to power—the Nancy Pelosi way is to respect that passion and bring power to truth.

The battle to take back the House in 2018 was an attainable but arduous one. The sexist and old question was looming over every single candidate running for Congress: Would you support and/or vote for Nancy Pelosi as leader of the House Democrats? Candidates were running in tough districts. Some had never even met Nancy—only seen the Republican caricature. Their consultants were eating up and believing everything Republicans and the Sheldon Adelson– funded Congressional Leadership Fund were spewing to the press: "Nancy Pelosi is going to be a drag on the congressional ticket." "It's better to ditch her." "Distance yourself." "Don't appear with her in public."

Nancy, on the other hand, couldn't have cared less about these sexist attacks. She didn't have any time to waste. With Republicans in complete control of Washington and determined to destroy people's health care and give billions in tax cuts to wealthy people and corporations shipping jobs overseas, Nancy was on a mission. She needed to strongly leverage House Democrats' power in the minority against Trump to bring control back to Democrats' hands and provide hope to millions of people devastated by the shocking results of the 2016 election. To that end, Nancy strategically and immediately fortified her alliances with key stakeholders, sharpening her decades-old grassroots expertise by holding weekly calls on mobilization efforts, teaming up with key allies to educate the American people about the Republican special-interest agenda, and traveling across the country to continue building the movement coalition.

Building strategic alliances as an individual member of Congress is one thing; using the convening power as leader or Speaker of the House is a much bigger kaleidoscope. By the time one gets to that level of power, there are layers of people to do the research, work on the issues, perform the outreach, and receive thousands of pieces of input. Nancy had long campaigned on being open and accessible to all of her members—smashing the marble ceiling herself to become Speaker, but also breaking down the hierarchies and formalities that historically made members of Congress (male and female) wait their turn to be heard, to offer amendments, to even meet with the Speaker. The woman who never had a meeting in the Speaker's office until she was elected Speaker now meets regularly with members in all configurations of the House Democratic Caucus kaleidoscope: freshmen, sophomores, constituency caucuses, issue area experts, and any member who requests a one-on-one sit-down. This allows ideas to percolate through the various channels of communication.

But she also needed to reinforce her unfiltered conversations with the advocates themselves—not to tell their stories but to hear them and to lend her microphone to their voices—because to succeed there must be a constant drumbeat of messaging. People need to see the faces of policy up front every day.

That is probably the biggest evolution in Nancy's leadership style. She has said her one regret about the efforts to pass the Patient Protection and Affordable Care Act was trusting other people to do the messaging. Now she does it directly with the stakeholders themselves. If other political actors join in, that's great, but the fate of her work lies in her hands, her caucus, and her microphone. She has always told the personal stories of the people she serves and brought them to speak for themselves, but now she attaches her sizeable platform with its social media reach as a force multiplier. Their colleagues can see them and believe that they have a seat at the table and the power to bargain for themselves. The explosion of nearly daily group engagement at the highest levels inside the capitol is a modern and welcome change we now take as a norm. The Speaker of the House, who never went to the Speaker's office until she was elected to the job herself, brings in advocates who could never before get an unfiltered audience with the Speaker to help write policy.

This open leadership is changing something fundamental about who gets to exercise their First Amendment rights to petition their government. Access is no longer limited to the lobbyists who know their work well and are paid well to petition. It is now open to grassroots advocates who aren't paid much but bring their invaluable experiences that draw connections between poverty, health and disability, systemic sexism and racism, ecological devastation, and immigration to the discussion of what it means to be the new suffragists bringing their "why" to the table.

Even—especially—because she is a leader, Nancy is connected to the team. When you are a leader, there is ambition on your own side and the opposition on the other, critiques from your own side and the criticisms from the opposition, all focused on cutting you off from your support. So rather than run alone, you need to be part of a team. Once people have invested in you, they want to see you attain the power to make the important choices and fight the good fight in a way that invites people to join. Now some people simply won't; they have a specific thing they want and will not help if they can't have it. Some did not want to save the Patient Protection and Affordable Care Act because they wanted to fight for single-payer health care. Some people did not want to fight for oversight and subpoena power unless they could say the word "impeachment." Others refused to commit to being on the team because they were running in very Republican districts and theorized that they would have more appeal if the act was bipartisan. But on some level everyone in a strategic alliance has at least one moment in the kaleidoscope where there is alignment and agreement—and that is the moment to organize them.

6

Know (and Show) Your Own "Why"

WHEN PEOPLE ASK NANCY WHY she serves in public office, she always answers in the same way: "Our children, our children, our children: the air they breathe, the water they drink, the food they eat, their health, their education, the job security of their parents and the retirement security of their grandparents. A beautiful, safe environment in which they can thrive and be healthy, and a world at peace where they can be safe and succeed and reach their aspirations. I keep working on it because it's like a horizon every time we achieve something we want to get closer to more. I see my own public service as an extension of my role as a mother and a grandmother."

Nancy knows her "why"—and she shows it in the legislation she champions to the activists she joins across the country and in San Francisco.

"It's all about the children and their education," said Nancy, surrounded by a large group of hardworking activists, educators, mothers, and public school students including her granddaughter Bella in San Francisco in May 2018 during a rally in support of Proposition G, a local ballot measure to raise public school teachers' salaries. Eloquently describing our fight that invests in hardworking educators during Teacher Appreciation Week, she proclaimed, "Teachers are custodians of our children's future, they help shape them, they help shape America."

The local fight was part of a national effort to fight the privatization of public schools by the Trump administration, whose Education Secretary had never stepped foot in a public school as a student teacher, parent, or administrator. The disrespect for public education and the looting of funds for special education and student wellness was a hot topic across the country with the "Red for Ed" movement, and at home: Nancy's daughter Jacqueline teaches art to special education students in Texas and her son-in-law Jeff teaches special education and walked out with his colleague protesting for decent pay and resources in Arizona.

Nancy's priorities in Congress for education include strengthening public schools, including through the "Better Deal" agenda of 2018 that would provide additional support to increase capacity in Title I schools and meet commitments to fund special education programs; providing loan forgiveness and lowering student debt, and enacting a comprehensive debt-free college plan; strengthening union rights and collective bargaining for basic workplace improvements, including higher wages and better working conditions; and supporting states and school districts in efforts to increase teacher compensation, retention, and resources. Various bills have been introduced to budget for more rights and resources while increasing oversight of the Department of Education and their policies putting lenders before loan borrowers, putting profits over public school educators, cutting hot school lunches and slashing eligibility even though everyone knows that hungry kids can't learn, and advocating for school nurses and wellness centers to help students. "It's about parents earning and children learning," Nancy says, often pointing out that many teachers and educators are parents themselves, and that their stress over high rents, undervalued wages, and insufficient classroom resources takes a toll on their capacity to be fully physically and emotionally present for their own children.

"It's all about the children and the job security of their parents," Nancy often says as she promotes an economic agenda for working families. Nancy's central theme, "When Women Succeed, America Succeeds," is based on an economic agenda of paycheck fairness, raising the minimum wage and tipped wages, union rights, small business tax credits, stopping wage theft, fighting sexual harassment, supporting pregnancy fairness, paid family leave, paid sick days, flexible schedules, quality child care with good pay and training for child care workers, and access to child support.[9]

Nearly everyone likes the sound of "When Women Succeed, America Succeeds"—it was the comment by President Obama that was rated most popular after the statement "Osama bin Laden is dead"—but each of the elements essential to that success has to be seen as valuable to men. This is not because men are doing women a favor but because all people need equity and all workers deserve the benefits of their labor and to not be "the only woman" in the meeting rooms, courtrooms, or boardrooms. As the leading family advocacy group MomsRising, and their Latina partner *MamásConPoder*, point out in their work, fair pay, work and family balance, and child care are as essential to helping the father as well as the mother. Simply put: To overcome sexism, we must address gender-based income inequality. The United States is terribly low in wage equality and in numbers of women in the legislative branch and in corporate leadership. The three are linked because political power is also manifested at the corporate board level. The same corporation making personnel decisions is also making political decisions through its political influence. Companies that don't promote women internally are not

---

9 "When Women Succeed, American Succeeds: Child Care." https://www .speaker.gov/sites/speaker.house.gov/files/migrated/wp-content/uploads/ 2015/05/Fact-Sheet-Child-Care-UPDATED-05-12-15.pdf

likely to support women leaders in office or women's policy objectives externally, either. From a candidate-recruiting perspective, more women in the C suites mean more women in the Congress. We know that this path is blocked by corporate libertarians fighting progress at every turn, giving lip service to women but not walking the talk on the fair pay, family leave, and childcare that are so essential to American families.

Nancy's agenda includes tackling racial disparity in earnings. Wage numbers are far lower for women of color—"white women make only 77 cents for every dollar earned by men, amounting to a yearly gap of $11,084 between full-time men and women," but "for African-American women and Latinas the pay gap is even larger. African-American women on average earn only 64 cents and Latinas on average earn only 55 cents for every dollar earned by white, non-Hispanic men."[10] Women, people of color, people with disabilities, and LBGT Americans confronted with wage gaps and employment discrimination will not earn as much as our straight white male counterparts without closing the pay gaps and passing the Equality Act to ensure that people cannot be fired simply for being gay, lesbian, bisexual, or transgender.

Nancy knows that these pay conversations are difficult to have. Over twenty years ago, Lily Ledbetter was never told that male managers with the same or less experience and responsibility as she had at Goodyear were being paid

---

10   World Economic Forum, "Global Gender Gap Report 2013." http://www3 .weforum.org/docs/WEF_GenderGap_Report_2013.pdf

more. When she sued for back pay and lost on a timing issue, Congress moved to change the law. Representative George Miller had followed the case and wrote the law eliminating the draconian notice and timing requirements, and Nancy got it passed and placed it on newly elected President Barack Obama's desk, where it was the first major bill he signed. (I saw Ms. Ledbetter at Nancy's 2013 National Women's Hall of Fame induction ceremony and said to her, "Imagine what Goodyear must be thinking—if only they had simply paid you what you were worth—instead you've helped millions of women and they've lost goodwill!") But women should not have to sue to get fair pay, Nancy argues; we should enshrine equity into law and business practices.

Part of why some men would rather see the "list" than elect women to implement it is because they didn't grow up with their mothers having any of these equities, and they don't have any substantial experience in valuing the work homemakers do. And that is why we need more women—and men—with a "why" like Nancy's to come change that culture and then change the laws. When Nancy went to Congress, her children were teenagers; however, now younger parents are running for office, and changing social norms are putting the pressure not just on the moms but on the dads to make substantial changes in how we treat employees, value work, and care for the caregivers. And the new generation of women Nancy encourages to come to Congress are making those changes now that they have the critical mass to do so.

Thus, the Fight for 15 Raise the Wage Act and the Fair Pay Act were passed in the first months of the 116th Congress. This push to raise the wage is about 30 million people—22 million of them women – getting a raise as a floor, not a ceiling. As Nancy said, in passing the bill "we always have to be anticipating and injecting fairness all the time. We must never stop fighting to honor the dignity of work and push forward for working families and women affected so drastically." Seeing moms and babies and caregivers and retail workers—women of color who led the fight for $15 as a minimum wage—sharing their leadership from the fast-food-restaurant picket lines to the speaker's podium with all the power it confers is a very substantial step forward in bringing people to the microphone who always have a voice, just not in the halls of power. At a September 2019 Equal Pay forum with Congresswoman Rosa DeLauro—the "godmother" of the congressional women's economic agenda—Nancy said: "Paying women less than men is an injustice. Paying women of color so much less than men is an exploitation that goes beyond injustice. That is why we pushed the For the People agenda to protect our health care including making sure that being a woman is not again a preexisting medical condition, and to give bigger paychecks—raising wages, passing equal pay, and increased equity for women-owned businesses."[11]

---

11 "Speaker in the House; Nancy Pelosi and Rosa DeLauro talk Equal Pay," September 14, 2019. https://www.facebook.com/CongresswomanRosaDeLauro /videos/979751259036232/

It's about the children, fighting for an AIDS-free generation. From day one, part of Nancy's "why" was clear: to fight AIDS. As she said at the AIDS Memorial Quilt 25th Anniversary Reception in 2012:

I went to Congress and they said you will be sworn in and because you're in the special election you will just be sworn in and that's it, and don't say a word because no one wants to hear a new member speak. So, I got sworn in, and the Speaker said: "Would the gentle lady from California like to address the House?" Oh my gosh, well alright, well the Speaker said so, members were saying "be very brief, be very brief, nobody wants to hear what you have to say." So, I went up there, was very brief, I thanked my parents who were there and my constituents who have sent me there and I said: "I told my constituents when I came here, that they sent me, and that I am here to fight against AIDS." Period. It was like ten seconds. It took me longer to describe it than to do it. So, I turn around thinking the folks that sent me there would say "perfect, you were very brief." Oh my God they were—"What is your problem?" I said: "I was brief, how much briefer could I be?" They said: "How on earth would you like to be identified here as the first thing you talk about being AIDS? Why did you say that you came here to fight against AIDS?" I said: "For a very simple reason: because I did. Because I did."

Her record is formidable. Among the highlights: bringing the lessons of San Francisco's model of community-based care, Nancy worked to accelerate development of an HIV vaccine, expand access to Medicaid for people living with HIV, and increase funding for the Ryan White CARE Act, the AIDS Drug Assistance Program (ADAP), the Minority HIV/AIDS Initiative, and other research, care, treatment, prevention and "search for a cure" initiatives vital to people living with or at risk for HIV/AIDS. She cowrote the Housing Opportunities for People with AIDS (HOPWA) initiative—an essential lifeline for people living with HIV and AIDS. To address the international pandemic, Nancy led the efforts to boost US funding for our bilateral AIDS initiatives that were in desperate need of international attention and vastly underfunded. Over the years, Nancy has challenged every presidential administration to fund treatment and research for AIDS, pushed for funding of hospitals and clinics as well as nontraditional treatments, medical marijuana, federal funding for syringe exchange, and lifting the travel ban for people with HIV/AIDS.

The Patient Protection and Affordable Care Act has provided significant benefits for those with HIV/AIDS by dramatically increasing access to Medicaid for people with HIV, improving Medicare Part D for people participating in the AIDS Drug Assistance Program (ADAP), ending discrimination based on preexisting conditions, and ending annual and lifetime caps on health benefits. Nancy participated in some of the earliest meetings for the NAMES Project AIDS Memorial Quilt, sewing her own patch for Susie, the flower girl in her wedding who died of AIDS, and helping to secure the needed permits from the National Park Service so that the AIDS Memorial Quilt could be displayed on the National Mall. In fact, "thanks to Pelosi's efforts, the NAMES Project was able to unfold 1,920 Quilt panels, representing more than 20,000 Americans who had lost their lives to AIDS or AIDS-related causes."[12] In 1996, Nancy led the legislation designating San Francisco's AIDS Memorial Grove, located in Golden Gate Park, as a national memorial. In addition to special anniversaries and workdays, Nancy has celebrated a number of anniversaries representing San Francisco by volunteering at the Grove. The street alongside the Grove, at the intersection of John F. Kennedy Drive and Martin Luther King Jr. Drive, is named Nancy Pelosi Drive in honor of her commitment to an AIDS-free generation and fight for LGBTQ equality and human rights for all.

Nancy sees the seeds of marriage equality in the early fight against AIDS and discrimination. Think of the strength of the community, she often says. As she elaborated in her 2012 remarks:

---

12 Jeffry J. Iovannone, "Nancy Pelosi: 30 Years an AIDS Advocate," *Medium*, January 29, 2018. https://medium.com/queer-history-for-the-people/nancy-pelosi-30-years-an-aids-advocate-50c026685439

The strength of this community and the model it was for the country. Everything we did legislatively: housing opportunities for people with HIV/AIDS, Medicaid if you had HIV and not full-blown AIDS, to be on Medicaid, every issue you can name in terms of the funding related to community-based solutions. We had the scientific geniuses that we all have here and that was important and they knew it was important to listen to the community. We had the care and the concern of people and San Francisco needed, even to the point of recognizing early on that if we're going to find a cure for HIV/AIDS, if we're going to address this issue, we had to have an international mobilization against AIDS. We were thinking globally because we knew that was what we had to do. And we came together with the pain, the suffering, the sense of community, the strength of this community, and the fact that we will keep fighting until there is a cure.

That bond inspired caregiving, policy making, and a fierce protection for each other's lives. The community was determined to find joy and family in the suffering. Once those bonds were formed, a network was there to push for human rights including housing, employment, military service, and marriage. Nancy often remarks that two of her first mentors in the LGBTQ community were Phyllis Martin and Del Lyon, who were a couple for fifty-five years. They taught her about lesbian health issues and bereavement challenges, and how important it was for the community to have the respect it deserved. Not coincidentally, they were the first same-sex couple to get married in San Francisco in 2004.

Her one regret is not yet finding a cure for AIDS. "If you told me then, 30-some years ago, that we would still not have a cure for AIDS today, I would have never believed you. . . . I thought we would have [it] within 10 years. While we have improved the quality of life, we still haven't eliminated HIV the way I would have hoped for."[13] And so the work for an AIDS cure and for LGBTQ human rights continues. As U2 rock star Bono said: "No one has fought harder than Nancy Pelosi since the day she came into office 25 years ago. Millions of people all over the world owe their lives to Nancy and the bipartisan coalition that fought to contain the AIDS epidemic."[14]

"For our children, a healthy environment." Nothing is more immediate to a parent than the air and water and food ingested by our children. Nothing is more central to our survival as a species than the protection of our environment. From her first days in Congress, Nancy was sent to fight pollution, protect the pristine coast, and improve environmental quality. Thirty years ago, Nancy passed the Pelosi Amendment that prohibited the US

13 John Riley, "Speaker Nancy Pelosi on celebrating Pride, advancing LGBTQ rights, and why everything in Trump's life is a cover-up," *Metro Weekly*, June 6, 2019, https://www.metroweekly.com/2019/06/nancy-pelosi-speaker-house-equality-act-pride-democrat-donald-trump/
14 Helena Andrews-Dyer, "Nancy Pelosi and U2: A Love Story," *The Washington Post*, February 28, 2019, https://beta.washingtonpost.com/arts-entertainment/2019/02/28/nancy-pelosi-u-love-story/

directors of the World Bank and multilateral development banks from approving loans unless there was an
environmental assessment made and made known to
the indigenous people locally, as well as internationally.
A report on the impact of the Pelosi Amendment went
into effect in 1991, and actions taken by the US government to implement it demonstrated that that environmental assessment and information access procedures
have been adopted and put into practice by all the major
multinational development banks, due in large part,
most observers agree, to the Pelosi Amendment. These
are widely credited with increasing the attention paid to
environmental concerns in projects, and with creating
greater environmental awareness and informal interaction between the bank staff and US officials.[15]

Nancy describes California and the San Francisco Bay
Area in particular as having a proud tradition of being a
"hotbed of bipartisan environmental fervor." It is where
John Muir established the Sierra Club, David Brower
established the League of Conservation Voters, and chil-
dren in grade school are striking for climate justice. As
Nancy said during her address to the September 2018
Global Climate Action Summit,

Combating global warming is not an issue. It is
an ethic. It is a value. And it is imperative that we

15   Jonathan Sanford and Susan R. Fletcher, "Multilateral Development
Banks' Environmental Assessment and Information Policies: Impact of the
Pelosi Amendment," February 12, 1998, http://congressionalresearch.com/98
-180/document.php.

act upon that value. For this reason, when I was Speaker [the first time], the priority of addressing global warming and energy independence was my flagship issue. Based on our values, informed by science—science, science, science—and inspired by the work of Vice President Al Gore, we created the Select Committee on Energy Independence and Global Warming, and passed the Energy Independence and Security Act, signed by President Bush: charting a new path to clean energy, reducing emissions, increasing the use of renewables and holding polluters accountable for environmental disasters.

Under President Obama, the House passed the Waxman-Markey American Clean Energy and Security Act, but it was stopped in the Senate by the coal industry.

Passing legislation to rejoin the Paris Climate Accords and raise efficiency standards on cars, and fighting the Trump administration's efforts to obliterate California's clean air auto emissions standards—Nancy is clear on her "why," as she said at the Climate Summit in September 2018:

We must act swiftly, boldly, and collectively in the face of a grim future, one of rising oceans . . . savage wildfires, and extreme and unpredictable weather patterns that devastate communities and destabilize our world. To confront the climate change,

Nancy grew up the youngest child of Thomas and Nancy D'Alesandro. Nancy has said that growing up with brothers Tommy, Nicholas, FDR "Roosey," Hector, and Joey prepared her to serve effectively in male-dominated political circles. *Courtesy of the Office of Speaker Nancy Pelosi*

A mischievous-looking Nancy with her family in the living room at 245 Albemarle Street in Little Italy Baltimore, where constituent service and political campaign activities were part of home life. *Courtesy of the Office of Speaker Nancy Pelosi*

Nancy doing homework with her mother, the First Lady of Baltimore, whose great love and wisdom has guided her only daughter. *Courtesy of the Office of Speaker Nancy Pelosi*

Mother
Dedicated to my Mother and all Mothers, Living and Dead

Mother, I think of you, Guardian Angel of my childhood.

Who can fathom the real meaning of the word Mother? Whose hearts are not filled with the memory of her, who has not stopped loving us from the first moment of our existence, when like a ray of sunshine that beamed down into our cradles! When the fingers of care and worry had not yet touched our hearts, it was Mother who was always around preventing their entrance into the holy island of Childhood.

Motherhood cannot be understood. It has its overtones in all languages; like magic it weaves a pattern full of joys, tears, patience, love, -- each exalting like music of golden bells.

Even when the word is spoken by an old man it sounds as if it comes from the lips of a child. To try to explain we must listen to our hearts as well as our minds. Mother teaches us to walk and play; to talk and pray. She knows the joys of happiness, she knows the sorrows of worry, care, and heartache. Mother is a beautiful person; when everything else in the world may change, she alone remains the same. Others may love us; but she knows us, understand us, and will forgive us whatever we may do. Mother is truly the living example of Christ's sublime Sermon on the Mount, for she had Fed the hungry, Given Drink to the Thirsty, Clothed the Poor, Visited the Sick, Buried the Dead, Taught the Ignorant, and has given Solace to the Sorrowful. In a few words Mother is God's Co-helper, and a radiant beam from the Mother of Mercy.

Words assembled by Nancy D'Alesandro

MOTHER—a poetic ode by Nancy's mother to her own mother. *Courtesy of the Office of Speaker Nancy Pelosi*

Nancy gave her first public speech at her father Thomas D'Alesandro Jr.'s inauguration as mayor: holding the Bible to swear him in and presenting it to him with these words: "Dear Daddy, I hope this holy book will guide you to be a good man." *Courtesy of the Office of Speaker Nancy Pelosi*

Nancy D'Alesandro and Senator John F. Kennedy at the 1958 United Nations Association of Maryland dinner in Baltimore. When the mayor's daughter met the Massachusetts senator, many people predicted that JFK would go on to be elected president of the United States, but absolutely no one could have predicted that Nancy D'Alesandro would go on to be elected the first and second woman Speaker of the House. Or that Nancy Pelosi would be awarded the John F. Kennedy Profiles in Courage Award by his family. *Courtesy of the Office of Speaker Nancy Pelosi*

Nancy and Paul Pelosi have been married for over fifty-six years—since September 7, 1963. Of their marriage, Nancy often says, "A successful marriage is a decision. You can't always be there but you have to be there enough and you always have to prioritize your family. My husband and I met in college. We couldn't have thought of every possible thing back then—we never could have imagined my going to Congress from California—but here we are. Every decision leads to another and every anniversary is an achievement." *Photo by Paul Morigi/ Getty Images for Ovation*

Nancy Corinne, Christine, Jacqueline, Paul Jr., and Alexandra in the early 1970s in Golden Gate Park not far from Nancy Pelosi Drive, a street which would be named for their mother forty years later. *Courtesy of the Office of Speaker Nancy Pelosi*

On April 7, 1987, Nancy won the Democratic primary for the US House of Representatives, placing her in a key position to win her first run for public office and to become the first woman to succeed a woman in Congress. The future Speaker's motto was prescient: "A Voice That Will Be Heard." *Courtesy of the Office of Speaker Nancy Pelosi*

On June 9, 1987, Nancy was sworn in as a member of Congress. Her father, Thomas D'Alesandro (seated), who had House floor privileges as a former member, accompanied her to the official proceedings and to this family photo with California Senator Alan Cranston in the Speaker's ceremonial office. *Courtesy of the Office of Speaker Nancy Pelosi*

A few months into her new job as US representative from San Francisco, Nancy marched in the "March on Washington for Lesbian & Gay Rights" in September 1987. *Courtesy of the Office of Speaker Nancy Pelosi*

True to her first words as a congresswoman, Nancy went to Washington to fight AIDS. She testified with her colleagues with actress Elizabeth Taylor, who served as the Founding International Chairman of Dr. Mathilde Krim's Foundation for AIDS Research (amfAR). *Courtesy of the Office of Speaker Nancy Pelosi*

With Senators Dianne Feinstein and Barbara Boxer, Nancy led the fight to protect the San Francisco Presidio from being sold to private developers and worked tirelessly for funding to clean up the waste from the former Army base and transform it into what she proudly calls the "crown jewel of the US Parks system." *Courtesy of the Office of Speaker Nancy Pelosi*

Nancy and Team Pelosi volunteers hard at work planting trees and landscaping the National AIDS Memorial Grove in Golden Gate Park, early 1990s. *Courtesy of the Office of Speaker Nancy Pelosi*

Nancy and then-San Francisco mayor Art Agnos briefed President George H. W. Bush about the devastating Loma Prieta earthquake of October 17, 1989. At that time Pelosi and Bush were engaged in a major legislative fight over trade policy with China after its government murdered human rights activists in Tiananmen Square on June 4, 1987; but notwithstanding those differences, Nancy secured significant Bush administration assistance to help rebuild her city. *Courtesy of the Office of Speaker Nancy Pelosi*

Secretary of State Hillary Clinton and Nancy Pelosi celebrated Women's History Month at the US Capitol in 2010. *Photo by Mark Wilson/Getty Images*

Supreme Selfie: Supreme Court Justices Elena Kagan, Ruth Bader Ginsburg, and Sonia Sotomayor join Nancy for an iconic Women's History Month group selfie. *Courtesy of the Office of Speaker Nancy Pelosi*

San Francisco Pride: Nancy has participated in over thirty LGBTQ Pride Parades, most recently with her supporters, children, and grandchildren in June 2019. The T-shirts feature her "clap" from the State of the Union; the rainbow wristbands serve as an ongoing homage to the Pulse nightclub victims murdered by a gunman targeting gay Latinos in June 2016 in Orlando, Florida, and the commitment to disarm hate. *Courtesy of Jorge Aguilar*

March 2010: Nancy applauded by staff after successful passage of the Patient Protection and Affordable Care Act, weaving health care into the American safety net. *Courtesy of the Office of Speaker Nancy Pelosi*

Summer 2013: Nancy and Paul celebrate their fiftieth wedding anniversary with Nancy Corinne, Jeff, Alexander, and Madeleine Prowda; Christine, Peter, Octavio, and Bella Kaufman; Jacqueline, Michael, Liam, Sean, and Ryan Kenneally; Paul Pelosi Jr.; and Alexandra, Michiel, Paul, and Thomas Vos. *Courtesy of the Office of Speaker Nancy Pelosi*

Nancy with His Holiness the Dalai Lama of Tibet, in Washington, DC. They have worked together for a generation. Nancy believes the role of a human rights activist is to "shorten the distance" between what authoritarians say is inconceivable and believers in freedom and justice know is inevitable. *Courtesy of the Office of Speaker Nancy Pelosi*

When Pope Francis spoke at the US Capitol, Nancy said, "He reminded us of our sacred and inescapable responsibility to those struggling to escape poverty, persecution, and war. He challenged us to rescue our planet from the climate crisis that threatens the future of our children and the health of God's creation—and to do so sensitive to the needs of the poor." *Courtesy of the Office of Speaker Nancy Pelosi*

January 2007: Nancy with then-Baltimore mayor and Maryland governor-elect Martin O'Malley in front of her childhood home on Albemarle Street, renamed "Via Nancy D'Alesandro Pelosi." *Courtesy of the Office of Speaker Nancy Pelosi*

Speaker Nancy Pelosi and President Barack Obama in her Capitol office. Together they passed sweeping legislation including the Lily Ledbetter Fair Pay Act, the auto bailout, Dodd-Frank Wall Street reform, the Recovery and Reinvestment Act, the Patient Protection and Affordable Care Act, the Fair Sentencing Act, and Don't Ask Don't Tell repeal. Obama has said, "The reason I love Nancy is because she combines a deep belief in making this country more just and more fair and better for our kids, with a toughness that is frankly unmet. . . . She knows to fight for her principles, but she also knows the importance of just getting stuff done." *Courtesy of the Office of Speaker Nancy Pelosi*

Photo by Chip Somodevilla/Getty Images

Top and Bottom: In 2007 and 2019, Nancy celebrated being sworn in as the first and second woman Speaker surrounded by her grandchildren as well as the children and grandchildren of Democrats and Republicans, saying both times, "For America's children, the House will come to order."

Photo by Mark Wilson/Getty Images

Election Night 2018: Nancy congratulated the "dynamic, diverse, incredible candidates who have taken back the House for the American people." She said the victory was about "restoring the Constitution's checks and balances to the Trump administration, honoring the vision of our founding fathers, the sacrifice of our men and women in uniform, and the aspirations of our children." *Courtesy of Jorge Aguilar*

Moment of victory: Nancy and supporters, including campaign director Jorge Aguilar (right), react to news that the Democrats had reclaimed the majority and won the House. *Courtesy of Jorge Aguilar*

"Women marched, women ran, women voted, and women won!"—Nancy in January 2019 posing with the Democratic women of the historic 116th Congress. Ninety-one Democratic women serve in Congress along with fifteen Republican women, making more than one hundred women serving in the 100th year of women's suffrage. *Courtesy of the Office of Speaker Nancy Pelosi*

A team that looks like America: Nancy with the Democratic Committee Chairs for the 116th Congress—a leadership that reflects the House Democratic Caucus, which is over 60 percent women, people of color, and LGBTQ Americans. *Courtesy of the Office of Speaker Nancy Pelosi*

"The times have found us" —Quoting American revolutionary and philosopher Thomas Paine, Speaker Nancy Pelosi delivered remarks announcing the House of Representatives is moving forward with an official impeachment inquiry against President Trump, September 24, 2019. *Photo by Alex Wong/Getty Images*

we must think globally, organize locally, and act personally—and that means understanding how to engage everyone in the solution, at every level of society, across all ethnic and community lines, including our indigenous people. For them, land is the gift of God and of their ancestors who rest there. A sacred place, a sacred place, with which they need to interact to maintain their identities and values. And we must also engage our young people because the future—this planet's future belongs to them. This is a top issue for millennials across the United States of America.

In September 2019, Nancy represented the United States at the G7 parliament meeting, where, despite Trump's pulling the United States out of international agreements, she pledged to keep fighting with boldness and urgency.

For our children, Nancy fights for a safe community free from the scourge of gun violence. Of all the things young people should have to worry about, being shot at school should not be one. But tragically, school shooting after school shooting has changed young people raised in what they themselves call "generation lockdown." The deadly shooting at Sandy Hook Elementary School in Newtown, Connecticut, on December 14, 2012 shocked the conscience of the country. Americans were horrified that twenty little first graders and six adults who threw their bodies over children to protect them were massacred in their classrooms. Almost overnight, groups were formed including Moms Demand Action—a Facebook page started by mom of five Shannon Watts that became a five-million-member advocacy group, assassination attempt survivor Congresswoman Gabby Giffords's Americans for Responsible Solutions (now Giffords Law Center), and the Newtown Action Alliance and Sandy Hook Promise. They came to Washington, DC, and mobilized for a federal bipartisan background checks bill that reached a majority in the Senate but lost in a filibuster and was never taken up in the Republican House. Vigil after vigil from California to Connecticut brought together new advocates with the organizers Nancy had fought with for years, dating back to her help in passing Senator Dianne Feinstein's Assault Weapons Ban of 1994; they include the Brady organization led by Sarah Brady after her husband Jim Brady was grievously wounded in the assassination attempt against President Ronald Reagan; Everytown, which had begun as Michael Bloomberg's Mayors Against Illegal Guns; local groups like San Francisco's chapter of Mothers in Charge, led by community leader Mattie Scott, who has been helping mothers of homicide victims for over twenty years after her own son was murdered breaking up a fight among his friends; and Survivors Empowered, founded by Sandy and Lonnie Phillips, whose daughter Jessi was killed in the Aurora, Colorado, movie theater massacre, a network of parents of gun violence victims who arrive on the scene after mass shootings to help the families navigate their grief.

As an organizer mom before going to Congress, Nancy could relate to the parents' work, saying in conversation with Shannon Watts at a March 2019 Women's History Month event: "When moms decide to band together to fight for our kids, think 'lioness defending her cubs.' We will do anything for our children. Being a mom, what are you? You're a diplomat, expert of interpersonal relationships. You're a chef. You're a chauffeur. You're a problem solver. You're a nurse. You're a health care provider. You have so much, and that's just with the children, not to mention the other aspects of family. And moms bringing those collective skills to an issue make us unstoppable. Knowing that moms are out there relentlessly shaping public sentiment toward common sense efforts to prevent gun violence and close the gun show loopholes gives me the power to negotiate knowing that moms will drive the public sentiment and deliver the voters."[16]

The groups began to co-organize, crossing racial and cultural divides, addressing the needs of urban communities whose gun violence was often blamed on crime and not its root causes and the lax gun laws, and breaking the silence of gun suicides, which are still all too often unreported. Nancy worked at building community among the 3 Bs—bibles (faith-based communities), badges (law enforcement and veterans), and business (socially responsible businesses)—needed for any bipartisan coalition. The massacre at Marjory Stoneman Douglas High School

---

16 Nancy Pelosi, Facebook video, March 16, 2019, https://www.facebook.com/86574174383/posts/10157506422404384?sfns=mo

on Valentine's Day 2018 shocked a Parkland, Florida, community into action and forced the country to listen to young people, because rather than having parents of young children speak there were high school students talking about their own experiences and mobilizing their peers. A month later, a group of young people—some of them survivors of the shooting—self-organized a "March for Our Lives" on Washington, DC. Nancy went to visit with them at their sign-making pizza dinner the night before the march. She told them that their march against gun violence with "persistence, insistence, eloquence, energy, and courage" reminded her of the civil rights march from Selma to Montgomery, which was begun by high school students. She told them,

> They were appalled that their parents didn't have the right to vote. What they did was insist, in a respectful way, that their teachers be registered to vote. And when they did that, they called attention to everything. The teachers did a boycott, and it caused a lot of attention. They said, "We are going to have a march over the Edmund Pettus Bridge; and we invite Martin Luther King and John Lewis." It turned into an international focus. And it made all the difference in the world. Now, you are high school students. You have an advantage that they didn't have: technology and social media. So, everything you do is to the nth degree immediately. You have the power to

mobilize in real time. And look at the result you
have produced already.[17]

Calling on them to be confident that she had their backs,
she said "I say to you what I say to my members: I would
rather win the vote on background checks and gun
violence safety protections than win the election. And
if Republicans won't do that, we have to change their
minds or change who's in office—because we must get
the job done. And I tell this to my colleagues: *There is not
a single person in the world whose political survival is more
important than the survival of our children.*"

Explaining the internal maneuvering and outside
mobilization, she invoked her favorite Republican president, Abraham Lincoln, who said, "Public sentiment
is everything. With it you can accomplish anything;
without it almost nothing."

They talked about organizing and mobilizing, and
Nancy reminded them that nothing is more eloquent
to a member of Congress than the voice of his or her
own constituent. She told them, "Tell a friend to call
a Republican if you don't have a Republican member
of Congress." And as they talked about the clear choice
between the NRA or the children of America, she urged
them to have faith that people would hear them.

The next morning, Nancy and Chef José Andrés

---

17 "Pelosi Remarks at Parkland Students' Pizza and Sign Making Party
Ahead of March for Our Lives." https://www.pelosiforcongress.org/2018/03/
pelosi-remarks-parkland-students-pizza-sign-making-party-ahead-march-lives/

were greeting marchers in the volunteer kitchen that was established to feed the marchers as they set off down the mall. In the weeks that followed, the young people not only joined the adults' organizational calls, but established their own calls and asked Nancy to call in and hear their updates and concerns directly from them—without adults or advisers filtering their views. Again, Nancy was at the heart of person-to-person storytelling, organizing, and nurturing to build community and make change.

The energy around these survivors in activism is heartbreaking and powerful.

Every day in the campaign and every day since the 2018 election there has been loss. So many mass shootings since Parkland—in 2019 too many more, especially in Gilroy, California; El Paso, Texas; and Dayton, Ohio, as well as the dozens of people killed by gun violence on the streets and in homes.

There are days when the pain is unrelenting. Every day in America over ninety families experience the agony of losing a loved one to gun violence. In late February 2019, House Democrats passed comprehensive bipartisan background checks bills and demanded a vote on them in the Senate. Unfortunately, Senate Majority Leader Mitch McConnell decided to block the bills in the Senate over the summer of 2019, even after the El Paso shooting that targeted Latinos, killing twenty-two people and wounding dozens more in a Walmart.

Nancy never gives up. She has been fighting this a long time, and the NRA has given her an F rating her entire career. But she has seen the public sentiment, the grassroots power, the local and state precedents to pave the way for federal reform. And now that the moms have joined with the teenagers, millions of Americans are telling the nation, "Enough is enough." Never bet against the moms—we are organized, mobilized, and determined to advocate for our children's safety. Someday soon there will be a change, and Nancy keeps showing her "why" with her organizing and legislating against these weapons of destruction.

Helping our children also means welcoming immigrant youth and respecting the beauty in the mix. A longtime champion of humane immigration reform, Nancy helped to develop and fund elements of the DACA—Deferred Action for Child Arrivals—program mechanisms that enabled young people who arrived in the United States as migrant children to register with the government and receive work permits and other documents to pursue education and jobs. A classic example of the "voice that will be heard" showing her "why" was the day Nancy decided to speak for the DREAMers during a fight over President Trump's decision to let DACA lapse, which threw the lives of millions of Americans into chaos.

It began innocuously as another day in the 115th Congress during which Republicans were rolling back Obama-era Wall Street reforms and undermining consumer protections. Representative Maxine Waters controlled the Democratic time opposing the financial services committee bill and yielded to Nancy Pelosi, who stepped forward to speak. While most debate and speaking time is limited, the leaders and the Speaker get a "magic minute," which is stated for the record as one minute but can last as long as they can talk without stopping. Nancy praised her longtime friend Waters for her service as the committee's top Democrat, spoke against the bill—"the cynically named Mortgage Choice Act provides anything but choice. Instead, it raises costs on consumers who have few alternatives. This is yet another attempt to stack the deck even further against working families."

But then she pivoted: "Mr. Speaker, this debate is another waste of time. Every day, courageous, patriotic DREAMers lose their status, and every day, the American dream slips further out of reach. As members of Congress, we have a moral responsibility to act now to protect dreamers, who are the pride of our nation and are American in every way but on paper. I use this occasion as opposing this bill to speak further about social justice in America."

And with that introduction, in four-inch heels, Nancy kicked off an eight-hour "magic minute" extolling the virtues of immigration, the need for humane reforms, and the demand for a path to citizenship. Nancy spent the next eight hours quoting scripture, telling stories, and explaining the contributions immigrants had made to America: nurses, educators, lawyers, activists, retail workers, caregivers, ROTC officers.

She quoted the Bible, Luke 10:25–37, the parable of the Good Samaritan, to evoke the justice of welcoming strangers. Samaritans were not friends to the person that the Samaritan saved, but he was a man of justice. She turned to the Founders: "'A new order of the ages,' it says, on the great seal of the United States, a new order, *'Novus Ordo Seclorum.'* That meant that it was predicated on the idea that every generation would take responsibility to make the future." She pointed to the rostrum, "In God We Trust," which it says there right over the Speaker's chair. Then she recited the Gospel of Matthew: "For I was hungry and you gave me something to eat. I was thirsty and you gave me something to drink. I was a stranger and you invited me in. I needed clothes and you clothed me. I was sick and you looked after me. I was in prison and you came to visit me. Truly I tell you, whatever you did not do for one of the least of these, you did not do for me." Then there were more stories about our DREAMers and why they honor the vows of our Founders, why they deserve our support.

The purpose of telling the stories was to illustrate the perils of ending DACA and terminating immigrants' work permits, financial aid, and military eligibility: "You can't have a Social Security card, a passport, a driver's license. You cannot function as a person in our society without having your status protected by the DREAM Act. So when people tell you it is all protected, it isn't. Listen to the stories." She made clear:

I am voicing some of the concerns today, largely through the voices and the stories of our DREAMers. We want to be sure that the public record of the Congress of the United States forevermore will reflect the stories of their great contribution to America in the hopes that those stories will move the Speaker of the House to give us a vote, to elevate this House of Representatives to its rightful place instead of diminishing us by saying the Senate may talk about these subjects that the American people care so much about, not so fast in the House of Representatives. So that is why I am using my leadership minute to make sure that the record will show the magnificent contributions of the DREAMers in our country, the courage it took for their parents to bring them here.

Quoting one young woman who wrote "DACA gave me wings, the wings I hoped for all my life when I was in school," Nancy said, "DREAMers are grateful for the mentoring they have received from people in our country, some of whom shared their heritage, most of whom did not. That is the beautiful thing about the DREAMers: they know that they have a dream, but somebody else had a plan for their own dream that inspired the DREAMers to have their plan."

Hours later, Nancy concluded:

Mr. Speaker, for the last eight hours, I have had the privilege of reading the testimony of so many DREAMers. I still have more, but I thank all of

you. It is a privilege to read the eloquent statements of the DREAMers as they express their love
of America, their commitment to a better future
for our country and their own families' better
future. It was a double honor to do so with the
recommendations of the testimony that you all
extended, presented, and to have so many of you
here in the course of the day, a real tribute to the
respect that we have for our DREAMers. Our basic
request is honor the House of Representatives.
Give us a chance to have a vote on the floor. Let
us thank and acknowledge the Dreamers for their
courage, their optimism, their inspiration to make
America more American.

The Democrats broke into applause, and Nancy turned
around to high-five her colleagues.

Reclaiming her time, Maxine Waters said, "Having
yielded one minute to the leader is the most profound
one minute probably in the history of this institu-
tion, that one minute that ended up eight hours where
Leader Pelosi talked about the plight of DACA and the
DREAMers."

The response was electric. People from all over the
country wrote in, called, emailed, texted stories to their
members of Congress, who then made them part of the
official record. "What it accomplished," Nancy told
the media afterward, "was to say we have our beliefs
and we're willing to fight for them and we're willing to

fight for them on the floor of the House." Although the Republicans did not relent, the courts did, and so the DACA program continues for now, although because it is "Deferred Action" the risk of deportations remain, and the millions of other immigrants need a path to legalization as well. Upon winning the House in 2018, all House Democrats and six Republicans passed the DREAM and Promise Act, which sets forth a blueprint for what that path looks like.

The lesson: know your why and show your why.

It may not be an eight-hour speech, but if it is real and comes from the heart, people will know that you care about them and want to lend whatever platform you have. In the days that followed, people reached out from all over the world to talk about the stamina, the commitment, and the clear love that shone through during the eight-hour magic minute—the longest speech on record in the House chamber.

People from around the world were calling and texting and tweeting. One lawmaker posted a photo of the four-inch heels. People knew Nancy was fighting for them. And an unintended benefit was that it sent an important message to the people saying she was too old for the job—"Let's see you try walking in her four-inch heels talking from the heart for eight hours straight!"

7

Know When to Weave and When to Whip

No one is a more reliable vote counter than Nancy Pelosi. Nancy has never brought a bill to the floor of the House of Representatives that she didn't win. The only bill she ever advanced that failed was the bipartisan Bush administration TARP vote where Nancy delivered the Democratic votes she promised, but the vote failed due to Republicans balking. She can give you an accurate vote count even when she is not whipping a bill—and especially when she is. What does it mean to "whip" a vote? The term itself is from fox hunting—the *Oxford English Dictionary* defines "whipper-in" as a huntsman's assistant who would whip dogs back toward the group—and the process caught on in British Parliament and then in the United States House of Representatives.

Nancy has developed a less violent image than a whip to put legislation together: when her colleagues elevated her to leader and Speaker. "I have a loom and I'm a weaver," she often says. "People say 'you hold your Caucus together so well!' And I say 'no, it's our values that bind us.' Every thread, every member of Congress, is a source of ideas, strength, and consensus for the policy we're trying to weave."

Meanwhile, just like back at home with the five kids, some people are spilling coffee on the tapestry or pulling out the threads or yelling that they'd like a better design or no tapestry at all. But she relentlessly cleans the stain, darns the frayed threads, asks for details and at least 218 votes for the new design, and keeps weaving. She sees the big picture that individual actors cannot. And whether she is weaving or whipping, she is always counting. No one else comes close to counting her votes and counting her blessings. When people ask, "Why doesn't she bring this for a vote?" the answer should be obvious: she has never lost a vote she wanted. If she had 218 votes, she would hold a vote. Until then, keep working.

As Nancy weaves her loom, the threads are coming from a variety of sources. Traditionally, the party leader is the person most responsible for the vote, but the network is vast and the elements of persuasion are complex. The reality is that the Nancy Pelosi way of whipping votes means looking not at hierarchy—remember the hierarchy that asked "Who said she could run?" when Nancy announced her intention to run for whip?—but at concentric and ever-widening circles.

The elected House Democratic Caucus hierarchy is one circle. The committee chairs and ranking members (as the highest-ranking members of the minority on each committee are called) know their members and how they have introduced, opposed, supported, or substituted legislation and amendments so they form a circle. Then there are other members who are former schoolmates, current DC roommates, House office building hall mates, election year classmates, elected from the same state mates, workout buddies, travel companions, or constituency caucus members who form another circle. Then beyond current members, there is the president and their staff, senators, governors, staffers, former staffers, party leaders, and friends in another circle. Then there is another whole sometimes overlapping circle of advocates and allies who push on the outside while members speak to each other on the inside. That set of circles involves volunteers, donors, advocates, pollsters, consultants, and individual constituents.

For each of the 435 members of Congress at the center of a vote, there are thousands of people in the surrounding overlapping circles, dozens of whom will be in contact with that representative at any given time. Most members want to be counted early so they can be part of whipping others. Some have genuine concerns that have to be talked through and worked out. Some people will get to yes with patience and conversations with "unusual suspects"—people who would not necessarily be on a whip list-keeper's radar, but who are threads in the weaver's loom because they are old friends from before Congress or from social or business experiences having less to do with the specific issue and more to do with what relationships with others or qualities in themselves matter to the members.

Nancy Pelosi tracks all of this. She continually asks each member about their district, their people, their needs, their ambitions and aspirations. And she talks to them over and over about those needs and weaves or whips votes accordingly.

While former House Speaker Tip O'Neill said "all politics is local," Nancy Pelosi says "all politics is personal." People taking personal responsibility for making the future better, for working with each other in a disciplined way, to make progress and fight the important fights, is deeply personal. Creating a community of love—"let other versions exist"—with people willing to work together is how Nancy weaves what she calls "the freedom of a tightly knit idea" in a diverse caucus. When people fight—and they always do—in private or in public, Nancy reminds them that they are a family and ultimately they have to decide to be a part of something larger than themselves, in coexistence with each other, united by their shared values, or not.

She has been in effect re-creating her family's famed "folder file" from Albemarle Street, where Little Nancy had written down the names of neighbors as well as their needs—get a job, get housing, get someone out of jail, get health care—and file it away, to be retrieved when someone else needed the same help and it was time to pay it forward. Nancy's list of legislative priorities, built on her own knowledge of who members are, whom they represent, and what they need to succeed in committee assignments and legislative craft, is a key ingredient of her success.

Over the years, Nancy's list has grown to an encyclopedia, but the little things are still the most important: detail and discretion. Every detail from personal touches like phone calls and handwritten notes to birthday wishes and get-well orchids, remembering that people are people and not politicians or donors or activists but actual soulful people, is an expression of empathy. Many people in politics love humanity but aren't as good at loving humans; the Nancy Pelosi way is to remember that people's hopes, dreams, and aspirations define them far more than the titles they hold, want, or held. Discretion is underrated but essential.

Former Congressman George Miller from Martinez, California, served as Cochair of the Democratic Caucus Steering and Policy Committee, top Democrat on the Education and Labor Committee, and author of some of the key progressive legislation for working families, children, and the environment in a forty-year congressional career. One of Nancy's closest friends in Congress, George logged thousands of hours on cross-country plane rides, conference calls, and informal conversations. He saw Nancy develop her deep and personal reservoir of knowledge about their colleagues. "There are leaders who don't know who they are leading," he says. "She does. She has a unique level of understanding of a member's district, family, supporters, and donors. She knows where they come from, who they sit with on the House floor, and what votes they consider to be their political liabilities. But that's the textbook. Presumably someone could have all that in a supercomputer and upload it into the cloud for storage: with Nancy it's all in her brain. What Nancy adds is intuitive knowledge about which of those resources to deploy, how to get the member to yes, and when to leave them alone with what can be a gut-wrenching 'okay then, we will talk tomorrow.'"

By "gut-wrenching" he means that the person knows they are in the circle of truth or consequences. They are among a small group of people she needs to reach a majority vote—generally 218 votes of 435. They know that Nancy will call again, and that they will likely be hearing from close friends and powerful allies in the meantime. "She doesn't get off the phone angry—she gets off the phone and plans the next step. Now it's time for the governor or college roommate or supporter to call. The conversation is left with unfinished business that is going to be finished."

Miller marvels at the way Nancy keeps everything close to the vest—even from her closest staff and colleagues. "We hear people spilling stories all the time—but

Nancy doesn't tell. People know that she doesn't talk. In my situation people would ask what happened—I would say 'I don't know.' One time she was counting cap and trade votes on a big climate bill and people kept telling her the votes were not there. Nancy didn't give up—said 'give me the list and leave me alone for a while.' Then she started calling. She never told us what she said as she worked with members to see the value of the climate vote, but she made sure her allies knew that we were going to help protect those yes voters once she did."

Whether she is weaving or whipping, Nancy is always counting. She knows what people need, what they love, what they fear—and she does not use it against them. She will not put people in a position of overwhelming liability if she doesn't have to. Over time, people understand her trust of other members. Miller emphasizes the self-discipline of discretion that makes Nancy effective: "This is a relationship between Nancy and each member. If the story is on the street, then everything is broken between them. She doesn't spill the details on how a member makes up their mind—or every resource she deployed to assist in persuasion because tomorrow is another day and Nancy and the Democratic Party will still need their support. Nancy simply says 'they came around' and leaves it at that. It's like the movie *JAWS*: all you really know about the shark is the music 'dun-dun dun-dun dun-dun-dun-dun.' But that's all you need to hear to know it's coming."

From working the front door of 245 Albemarle Street

at age ten, Nancy learned a lot about people, and she remembers nearly all of it. She remembers conversations, lessons, political races, legislative horse trades, electoral outcomes, and emotional experiences. And she never tells. She does not trade in gossip—to the disappointment of those wanting to hear the juicy nuggets about famous people's foibles—and advises against learning too much about a situation lest the confessor move away from the confidence out of embarrassment. Handling people's secrets really is a trust, and allowing people the space to let every day be a new day is a special skill in restraint. I can remember a story she told me about a woman she knew in the 1970s who was having man troubles. The woman revealed lots of information about the man, then reconciled with the man, and stopped being close with Nancy. The lesson: don't take on too much of someone else's drama—and definitely don't trash the person harming them. "Ever had a friend who's dating a jerk?" she will ask. "You can't tell them the person is a jerk, because they'll defend their choice. All you can do is point out some broken promises or how unhappy your friend is and hope they reach their own conclusions." This is also good advice politically for dealing with ticket splitters who may have voted for a certain president who brought them pain instead of greatness.

Since the objective is to weave a party position through threads of consensus, it is beyond frustrating when people decide to contribute to the process and then decide to trash the decisions of the group or give their vote to the president of the other party. At one point during the George W. Bush administration in the early days of the Nancy Pelosi leadership, some members announced that they had promised their vote to the president. Her response to the caucus, when these situations would arise: "If a Democrat asks to be relieved of your commitment to the Democratic caucus because it is a matter of conscience, we accept that. But if you ask to be relieved of your commitment to us so you can give the Republican president your vote, don't be surprised when the Caucus asks to be relieved of its commitment to you." Sometimes people will not commit at all, and at other times they will not take kindly to being told their opposition is not appreciated.

People are human and don't always hit the weave or whip note. Being ready for the possibility of disappointment is part of the process. There are often so many public whip lists and social media tags in the feeds of legislators (most of whom do not do their own social media or try to mute conversations so they can engage without being sucked in to a vortex), so the rules of technological interaction are changing how people relate. Some people are just very uncomfortable being publicly undecided. You don't want to be the last member straggling up the Capitol steps trailed by reporters who all want to know what you will do. Commit when you know, so the team can redirect resources elsewhere. Nancy's strength is that she hits the mark more often than anyone and understands the very personal way people respond to how they are weaved or whipped. As she puts it bluntly: "In Baltimore, I learned how to count. And that is really what serves me in a good stead, whether it's about my own election or my election to leadership or my passing legislation. You really have to know how to count and what is 'yes,' and what is 'that would be nice.'" Considering that, as former congressman David Obey famously said, "The only people you can trust in this place are those who look you in the eye and tell you they are voting against you," the interpretation of data in all those circles of engagement and compassion is essential to a result. And as George Miller said, "Many people can engage with credibility. You can make an argument to members why they should be and have to be yes. What Nancy adds is the affirmation: 'You know you can do it.' I've seen us all take tough votes together but I've never seen her throw anyone to the wolves."

Never was that more true than during the fight for health care in 2009 and 2010. As the Kennedy Library told it when giving her the John F. Kennedy Profiles in Courage Award:

In 2010, amid a public climate of deepening polarization, Nancy tirelessly spearheaded the passage of the Patient Protection and Affordable Care Act. The PPACA has subsequently enabled millions of Americans to have access to quality, affordable health care, and improved benefits for tens of millions more; it was the most significant expansion of health care access since the implementation of Medicare and Medicaid nearly half a century before. Following its passage, Pelosi became the subject of negative political attacks from the GOP. Democrats lost control of the House in November 2010, ending her first tenure as House Speaker.[18]

The weaving and whipping process around health care was excruciating. Deals would fall apart, and momentum in the Senate stalled as people chased a bipartisan deal that was sadly not forthcoming. House members were verbally abused at town halls by people who ranged from genuine concerns to such remarks as "Keep your government hands off my Medicare." (Maybe they did not know that Medicare is government, or maybe when they like a program it's not government in their minds.) Whatever the case, every time something changed in one part of the bill, Nancy risked losing votes in another part. There was a bloc of anti-choice House Democrats who threatened to bring down the whole bill, so the agreement was to pass a sweeping bill with a restriction that would be removed in compromise with the Senate.

When Nancy said, "We have to pass the bill so that you can find out what is in it—away from the fog of the controversy," she was attacked relentlessly by people

---

18 "U.S. House Speaker Nancy Pelosi to Receive the 2019 John F. Kennedy Profile in Courage Award," April 7, 2019. https://www.jfklibrary.org/about-us /news-and-press/press-releases/2019-profile-in-courage-award-announcement

opportunistically claiming that the process was secret (it wasn't), that it was too fast (it took months), or that Democrats didn't know the contents (they did).

But in the end, Nancy was correct. People support all the patient protection aspects of the bill, including a ban of lifetime limits on insurance coverage, a ban on rescission or retroactive canceling of an insurance policy which companies used to dump patients, a guarantee that young adults could stay on their parents' health insurance plans up to the age of twenty-six, guaranteed coverage of a full menu of preventive health-care services, and a guarantee that insurance companies actually spend most of their revenue on health care with a rebate to customers if they don't.

However, at the time, the media and Republican attacks were ferocious. People claimed that the bill contained death panels or did nothing to restrain health-care costs—both demonstrably false but obscured in that "fog of controversy."

But Senator Ted Kennedy died, and although his temporary successor Paul Kirk cast the vote to break the Senate Republicans' filibuster, the Democrats lost the special election for the seat, dooming the effort's chances. Republican Scott Brown had driven a pickup truck the length and breadth of Massachusetts opposing the health-care plan, which was actually built on his state's model of universal care as implemented by Republican governor Mitt Romney. A struggling economy haunted people still coming out of the 2008 market crash and Republican recession, and their anger was palpable. It was sadly ironic that Brown won the seat held by Kennedy, who had spent his life fighting for health-care reform. Election night crowds cheered "Forty-one!" in reference to the forty-first vote Brown would give Republicans in the Senate to filibuster the health-care bill. Brown claimed, "People do not want the trillion-dollar health care plan that is being forced on the American people." Senate Minority Leader Mitch McConnell said, "They don't want this bill and want Washington to listen to them."

Even some Democrats were ready to throw in the towel, saying we could not break the filibuster, so should try for a smaller-scale bill or wait for Brown to be seated and start over with a new approach to health-care reform. Not Nancy. "We don't say a state that already has health care should determine whether the rest of the country should," she said on election night. "We will get the job done. I'm very confident. I've always been confident." In that darkest of hours, she insisted we will "push through the gate" because "we must pass health care reform. The problem is still there. The financial aspects of it, the cost to individuals, to their families, to small businesses, to big businesses, to all businesses, to our deficit, to our federal budget and to our economy are huge. . . . We cannot sustain financially the current system so this has to take place. The fact is also that, as long as people are discriminated against because they have a preexisting condition or their policies are canceled because they get sick or their procedure is denied on the way to the operating room with rescissions, as long as people go bankrupt if they have a diagnosis, we must pass this legislation. And we must take whatever time it takes to do it. Some things we can do on the side, which may not fit into a bigger plan. That doesn't mean that is a substitute for doing comprehensive. It means we will move on many fronts, any front we can." After pointing out that people were paying too much for care, living in fear of being cut off during treatments, and discriminated against for having preexisting medical conditions from cancer to having birthed children, Nancy reiterated her determination to make systemic change, with other fixes to come after the major guarantees and coverages were put in place. She vowed, "We will go through the gate. If the gate is closed, we will go over the fence. If the fence is too high, we will pole-vault in. If that doesn't work, we will parachute in. But we are going to get health care reform passed for the American people."

For the next three months, most did not share her confidence. On many days, no one but Nancy Pelosi thought the votes were there. And there were people on the president's staff who thought sweeping health-care reform was too hard and that President Obama should retreat and return with a child-only health-care bill. But Nancy told President Obama and his staff that she would not accept what she called "Kiddie Care" and insisted on a bigger bill, knowing that it meant a tough and risky fight. She rejected any "eensy, weensy spider, teeny tiny" bill and insisted that Democrats should finish the job

Ted Kennedy had called "the cause of our lives." She kept doubt from her mind so she could weave and whip the caucus as needed.

She pushed back on people disappointed that the Senate bill removed her public option and on certain Catholic lawmakers who threatened to vote no once their abortion restrictions were not in the Senate bill. She worked with pro-choice lawmakers who opposed restrictions on insurance coverage of abortions. She talked with the unions who hated the Senate's tax on high-cost health plans whose benefits were bargained for in lieu of cash or pensions. Meanwhile the political heat kept coming with more and more doomsayers—and more and more Democrats telling her they did not see a path forward—but Nancy kept focused and positive, telling people it would pass because the country needed historic, fundamental change.

As former Congressman George Miller remembers, this was a career-defining vote of courage. Nancy made it clear that she knew they were all taking a vote of courage. "She had a very small pool of people," he recalls, and the bill could have gone down due to the lawmakers who did not like the Senate taking out the public option or to the anti-choice lawmakers who did not like the Senate taking out their abortion restrictions.

Nancy persisted, reminding members of her caucus that Democrats had been fighting for universal coverage for decades—and that even a flawed bill was worth passing, especially because it would be possible to amend and improve the law later on, just like previous generations of lawmakers had done with Medicare, Medicaid, and Social Security.

At one point, Nancy, Senator Harry Reid, and President Obama agreed upon the path but the votes were missing. Aides brought in a list of 68 members of Congress. Nancy did not flinch: "I'll take all 68," she said. She would need all of them. The "Winter Soldiers" coalition of outside groups from labor unions to patient advocates had constant calls and check-ins with the House and the White House. Everybody knew the stakes: they could lose if they voted yes and they could lose the chance for health care if they voted no or scaled down the bill.

Ultimately, says George Miller, "Nancy convinced wavering members that expansions of access and improvements to care were more important than what they disliked; that the other changes could be made later but were not worth ending the only chance we had" to add health care to the American social safety net. This was a fight one hundred years in the making, and one election in a state with universal health care was not going to change that—if anything it was grist for motivation: why punish everyone else because some (not all) Republican voters in one state had theirs and wanted to deny everyone else? Failure was not an option: she tried and tried with her grassroots arm of patients and advocates who trusted each other and trusted her.

"This was never thought to be easy," Nancy said before the vote. "It doesn't matter what we're saying here. What matters is what happens at the kitchen table of the American people, and how they will more affordability, more accessibility, better quality care, prevention, wellness, and a healthier nation. We must pass the bill."

Pass it she did, with cheers in the House gallery and across the country.

The lesson: You need to weave and whip to reach a hard count. You have to know your why and the why of each person whose vote you are counting. Take whatever you think you have and subtract 30 percent. The fudge factor isn't all treachery. People make multiple promises or change their minds or think someone else with less political risk can take the vote or you may not need them and don't want to hold them if there's a chance you can win without them. This is where interpreting data and using compassion come in. Sometimes someone cannot form the "ask" to tell you what it would take to get them where you need them, so be patient when you can and allow yourself a chance to circle back with that phone call or follow-up visit that may turn the tide. While many an advocate would prefer a strong-arming party boss to enforce an action, the reality is that people don't work that way. Elected officials have their own whys, their own careers, and their own judgments about when they will support the Democratic Party. Scorched-earth whipping is the worst on everyone, and sometimes people care more about how you treat them than about the substance of an issue. To paraphrase Maya Angelou, people may forget what you say but not how you make them feel.

So give the interaction the space to leave people to enter a coalition or a vote in their own way. Other times you need to whip a vote to hold together as a unit or political party. An iteration of this message is woven into nearly every big vote: We are a family and we respect votes of conscience, but you can't expect loyalty if you betray us for the person who is trying to harm the people we serve. And we accept it may get messy from time to time when the voting gets rough. But political risk is part of the "why." As Nancy said repeatedly when asked if she had any regrets about losing her Speakership over passing health care: "I came here to do a job, not to keep a job."

8

Remember, Criticism and Effectiveness Go Hand in Hand

IF THERE IS ONE ELEMENT to standing her ground that Nancy Pelosi does better than anyone, it's forging through a storm of criticism with clarity and spirit.

Nancy has drawn upon the discipline to be herself as a member of Congress applying what she defines as "constituency, Constitution, and conscience" to set a moral compass and, if necessary, take on the president of the United States. She has served during the Reagan, George H. W. Bush, Clinton, George W. Bush, Obama, and Trump administrations, has worked with all of them, and has taken principled positions in contrast to policies proposed by each of them.

A few examples:

Nancy fought for AIDS to be seen as a public health epidemic and to get the same kind of research and treatment dollars that cancer and other diseases got. The early years of institutionalized homophobia by the Reagan administration cost thousands of lives.

She brought her voice to ending aid to the Contras fighting in Nicaragua and to promoting peace in Central America. In fact, her June 9, 1987, swearing-in day coincided with the hearings that exposed Reagan's Iran Contra arms for hostages scandal that forever tinged his presidency.

In June 1989 when the Chinese government sent tanks to crush a student-led pro-democracy movement, she immediately stood up in opposition to the oppression and brought forth bills to protect the Chinese students in America and to deny most-favored-nation trade status to China, contrary to the wishes of the George H. W. Bush administration. That began a career-long relationship with dissidents and democratic reform movements in Tibet, Hong Kong, and Taiwan. A few months after the massacre in Tiananmen Square, the 1989 Loma Prieta earthquake rocked San Francisco. The city was damaged, the people were scared, and the Marina District would be without power for days. Putting other differences aside, Nancy worked with President George H. W. Bush to bring emergency relief to the city. She made sure that her constituents received timely assistance, joining her California colleagues to secure a $3.45 billion earthquake relief package, raising the Small Business Administration loan cap to help people start over, and leading efforts to restore civic landmarks like City Hall and the Geary Theater, home of the American Conservatory Theater, as well as neighborhood streets and parks.

Nancy worked hard to elect President Bill Clinton and Vice President Al Gore, serving as the 1992 platform cochair and helping California swing from Republican to Democratic for the first time since 1964. In one of her proudest legislative achievements, after the Army closed the Presidio of San Francisco (which had been a military post from 1776 to 1994), Nancy joined Senators Barbara Boxer and Dianne Feinstein to lead the fight to preserve the Presidio for the people of San Francisco against those planning to sell off this treasured asset to the highest bidder. In 1996 she passed a bill that President Clinton signed creating the Presidio Trust, with the twin goals of preserving the essence of a magnificent national park and achieving economic self-sufficiency. Today it is the crown jewel of the parks system, with the Walt Disney Family Museum, Futures without Violence, Letterman Digital Arts Center, Japanese American Historical Society, and the transformation of Crissy Field from a barren waste site to a recreation site. But when she disagreed with President Clinton, Nancy took action, waving a protest banner in Tiananmen Square during a 1999 visit to the consternation of the Chinese government, and vocally opposing the Defense of Marriage Act, the Crime Bill, and so-called welfare reform.

Nancy opposed President George W. Bush's 2001 tax cuts, but their biggest schism came after September 11, 2001. It was a cruelly beautiful sunny day when the workday began, and the odd news of a plane hitting one of the New York City World Trade Center twin towers turned to terror when the second plane banked its wings and hit the second tower. All of Capitol Hill was evacuated, with members and senior staff being briefed offsite at the Capitol Police station. Tanks in the streets, smoke rising from the Pentagon fire, and news of a downed plane in a Pennsylvania field crashed intentionally by courageous passengers who knew the plane was headed for Washington, DC.

By midday a harrowing, horrifying reality was setting in. Thousands were killed, millions were terrified, and we did not know if more attacks were coming. I was working on Capitol Hill that day for John Tierney of Massachusetts, who had constituents on two planes hijacked from Boston's Logan Airport. We were at an ad hoc House Democratic Caucus meeting, stunned, angry, and defiant. Nancy—then a top Democrat on the intelligence committee—was among those who insisted that Congress return to the Capitol that day to show that the terrorists did not "win"—though they murdered thousands of us, they would not have the rest of us cowering in fear. In the early evening of September 11, 2001, members of Congress, staff, and families convened at the

Capitol. We took heart from vigils around the world, and headed to our own vigil with leaders, staffers, and press back across the Capitol esplanade. Already concrete barriers, military vehicles, and security unseen since the 2001 inauguration had been set up around the Capitol, some permanently. By dusk, hundreds of people gathered to join a defiant, unified vigil of leaders on the Capitol steps singing "God Bless America."

When the national moment of unity did not last, Nancy took on the Bush administration and insisted on an independent probe into the terrorist attacks.

Former congressman Tim Roemer of Indiana remembers the fight: "Both Nancy and I had proposed legislation to establish an independent 9/11 commission. One day she spoke to me in the cloakroom, said, 'go with yours instead of mine because you can get more votes across the aisle than I can'—she is visionary in who is going to get it done, not caring who will get the credit for it." Roemer recalls a momentous meeting with White House aides where he, Nancy, and Senator John McCain were pushing reforms but the White House aides kept putting off the 9/11 Commission creation. Several 9/11 family members were in the room. "They stood up and said 'no more stalling—give us an answer right now. Tell us to our faces.' Nancy, John McCain, and I sided with the families." Bush came on board, but things almost went off track the next year when he nominated controversial former Secretary of State Henry Kissinger to be the Republican cochair. In the uproar that followed, Nancy demanded that everyone on the commission reveal their client list. The conservatives were howling and blasting Nancy but she remained firm, Kissinger withdrew, and Thomas Kean got the position instead. The Commission made forty-one unanimous bipartisan recommendations, thirty-eight of which were adopted into law. The criticism was worth the result—progress, as well as prevention of a large-scale attack of that size ever since.

While serving as House Democratic Whip in 2002, Nancy bucked Leader Richard Gephardt's support for Bush's war in Iraq, and led 155 House Democrats (over half the caucus) to support the John Spratt amendment to continue negotiations. At the time, many Iraq War supporters in Washington, DC, viewed the vote on the Iraq War as a test of who had the toughness to be the next leader of the Democrats. It was true—but not in the way they intended, and Nancy's view became the majority view in the Democratic Party and in the country.

Despite objections from some in the Bush administration, Nancy helped write and pass laws establishing the Office of the National Director of Intelligence and a whistleblower law for the intelligence community, and together with Intelligence Committee colleagues like Roemer helped diversify the human intelligence workforce to look more like America and enable them to be more effective around the world. Once again, criticism was the price Nancy was willing to pay for being effective and making changes she saw as vital to her responsibility to protect and defend the Constitution and the country.

Nancy worked as President Obama's strongest ally on Capitol Hill, enacting laws from fair pay to reinvestment and recovery to Don't Ask Don't Tell repeal, passing budgets, and sustaining his vetoes throughout his second term. When she placed the Patient Protection and Affordable Care Act on Barack Obama's desk, it was after she had vigorously fought his administration when his chief of staff wanted to settle for far less than sweeping care for millions of Americans. And in February 2012, Nancy vocally supported freedom to marry in the national Democratic platform, having already endorsed it years before, and urged President Obama to say that he supported equality in marriage. It took a few months, but Obama did eventually "evolve" on the issue, and the following year the United States Supreme Court agreed.

Starting before Donald Trump was sworn in, Nancy called for an independent investigation into his relationship with Russian interference in our elections during December 2016 when some of members of the Electoral College—myself included—demanded a briefing and reclassification of the intelligence so that we could deliberate, as Alexander Hamilton intended in *Federalist Papers* 59. (We "Hamilton Electors" did not get the briefing, but the American people got the Mueller investigation and congressional oversight.) She then led the Our First Stand rallies across America to protect the Patient Protection and Affordable Care Act. From their first meeting of his presidency, when he used the occasion to tell congressional leaders, "You know I won the popular vote because three to five million people voted illegally—and I'm not even counting California," and Nancy had to break protocol to say, "Mr. President, that is not true. That is not true. What you are saying has no evidence, no data, no truth, no fact to it," she knew it was going to be a series of contentious engagements.

Trump promised an infrastructure bill at that meeting—"I have the plan right here. It's a trillion-dollar plan, and we can pass it right away. Right, Mitch?" McConnell said, "Not unless it's paid for." And that foretold McConnell referring to himself as the grim reaper, claiming the Senate was a legislative graveyard for health care, jobs, climate action, gun reform, and ethics—pretty much everything except corporate tax cuts and the confirmation of conservative corporate judges. Still, the occasional reform bill or veterans affairs or appropriations bill gets through, including the deal to end the shutdowns and raise the debt ceiling for two years. There is an outside chance Trump will comply with court orders to enforce subpoenas, but if not, additional accountability will come his way with every decision in the impeachment inquiry resting on the merits, not the politics or the pundits or the legions of people criticizing Nancy rather than rounding up the currency of the realm: 218 votes.

None of these presidents have appreciated the criticism. They thought they were right and that Nancy was not, and they used their allies in the media, in the public, and in the Democratic Party to try and undermine her. But she was ready for the attacks, for the undermining, for the snubs from the Republican presidents and from the Democrats. It took a while for the presidents to realize that Nancy sees Congress as a coequal branch of government that works *with*, not *for*, the executive branch and the judiciary. She has sat in meetings at the tables of power and told presidents to their faces that they were wrong or that they didn't have the votes from her members. Try as they might to cajole or undermine, she does not let that get under her skin. And she is perfectly comfortable disagreeing on one issue and working out the others for the sake of governing America.

From president to president, where Nancy can, she finds common ground, and where she cannot, she stands her ground. In each instance, holding her own and being true to herself has meant being able to withstand nasty criticism and pressure to slow down or speed up or sit back or step aside. With the thousands of little decisions that go into making big choices, Nancy Pelosi is consummately prepared, ready to take the heat, and able to shrug off personal attacks in order to win on policy.

Much has been made of attacks by Trump. Nancy is not moved: "The president has been a projector." She says, "Every time he calls somebody something, you know he's projecting his own diagnosis. Whether it's lazy, whatever it is, he's just saying, 'I know this is what I am, so before somebody identifies me this way, I'll identify them that way.' So I don't really care about what he says. And again, I got him very hurt when I said he was guilty of a cover-up. Everything in his life is a cover-up.

The term 'cover-up' hit directly home with him, and I think that's what triggered his response, which was to turn on me what he projected to be his own diagnosis."

"This is not for the faint of heart," Nancy often warns candidates. As a party leader, she is at the center of every fight. That means by definition that someone—probably by an ally—will criticize her every hour. Social media multiplies the snarly messages and drowns out the positive praise or nuanced discussion, so it is highly likely that whatever you are reading about an issue bears little resemblance to what is actually happening behind the scenes.

How in the world does she do it? She remembers that effectiveness and criticism go hand in hand.

Here are some insights: Nancy is not moved by personal insults and does not internalize them. Whether she is attacked in one ad or 137,000, a personal insult will not move her on an issue—actual votes from her members and constituents do. Whether an insult tweeted by the president or a fake "drunk" (Nancy doesn't even drink!) video that Facebook allowed to circulate to millions of users, Nancy keeps her cool and doesn't take the bait. She declutters her mind from distractions, speaking in shorthand and simply changing the conversation to "how are your children?" when she's had enough. She eats chocolate ice cream for breakfast and reads in the bath at night. She does not go to the gym but prefers long and very brisk walks in her beloved Presidio or along the Potomac. She loves to dance (well) and sing (not so well), and, although she raised her kids with long drives around Northern California playing cassettes, she doesn't have much time to listen to music unless she is at the show itself. She loves live performances and often says the arts are what can bring America together no matter how trying the times.

She has strong executive decision-making skills, preferring to "touch it once" when it comes to paperwork rather than revisit memos and requests inefficiently. She carried the mantra her children have heard since childhood, "proper preparation prevents poor performance," into her congressional offices. She insists on time away from politics to connect with family and friends. She and Paul are still very close with their college roommates from Trinity and Georgetown, and Nancy often sees her older brother Tommy, still her fiercest defender and critic. She will advise people obsessed with a political event to "put it on the shelf" and clear their head. She listens more than she speaks, and she speaks views that people sometimes don't want to hear. Nancy has retained her sense of self and purpose despite the hundreds of millions of dollars spent in hundreds of thousands of negative ads aired against her over the years. No matter what they throw at her, she is resolute.

Although there is never enough compassion in scheduling—the work is a grind and every appearance requires a sharp, engaged presentation—she logs hundreds of thousands of miles eating cheese out of a snack box perched in a middle seat on plane after plane after plane because that's what it takes to be effective. When Nancy travels across the country, she is present in each space—remembering friends, connecting with the community, and listening for people's storytelling of their why. She organizes her outfits by the trip since she will be in at least two if not six cities a week, makes sure her clothes are fresh when she gets to each hotel room, and irons them if they are not. At one particularly contentious California Democratic convention Nancy arrived, calmly ordered room service, and began unpacking. Between bites of a club sandwich she ironed her shirts as we were briefing her on the tough votes ahead—a scene not unlike the 1970s elementary school days when she would be pressing uniforms and receiving homework reports.

Nancy loves representing San Francisco and says of the ads dismissing her and her city: "To those who mock me for having 'San Francisco values,' which is their code for being pro-LGBTQ, I say, 'We don't tolerate our differences—that's condescending. We take pride in our diversity. And when it comes to full social equality, the inconceivable to you is the inevitable to us. Listen to what we say because pretty soon you'll be saying it too.'"

Her personal pain threshold to withstand billions of dollars' worth of attacks from the right along with untold hours of corporate media criticism and a drumbeat of insistence tinged with misogyny from some on the left is steeped in her "why"—the one in five children living in poverty, and insistence that we put people's needs and dreams first. She simply does not give up. She does not

stop organizing and finding a way to shake the kaleidoscope to bring new perspective and fresh thinking to a
problem. She remembers everything without needing to
write details on a card in a file but doesn't mention it or
trade in gossip, leaving space for tomorrow to be a new
day.

She quotes a line Phil Burton used to say: "They'll
understand when they understand." And no one has
more ability to wait it out than Nancy Pelosi. She will
ask for a vote or a donation and pause as long as it takes
for an answer—not breaking into uncomfortable silence
to bet against herself. She is big on "keeping the friendship in your voice" and building relationships big and
open enough to disagree without losing respect for the
authentic perspectives people bring. Ask some of Nancy's
adversaries turned allies and they'll say she listened to
them tell her in painful detail what they didn't like about
Congress or her or Congress led by her—and in so doing
became her trusted confidants precisely because she
welcomed their honesty, absorbed angry conversations,
negotiated solutions and compromises, and kept on task.

As Congresswoman Anna Eshoo puts it: "When
Nancy is on the road to where we need to go, you can
honk, you can tailgate, you can speed—but you can
never knock her off track; she stays on course, she keeps
going on her path; she refuses to lose focus."

She is keenly aware of the corrosive effect of negative campaigning: "I do think that the Republicans have
made it more mean-spirited by their politics of personal

destruction. I think that started in the 1990s and it was very destructive. And then in the 2000s, the difference has been one of communications. To be able to communicate in real time has its pluses and minuses—the minus being you don't have a lot of time to check out the facts before people are putting things forward."

Having seen the impact of those attacks up close, I don't know of any party leader anywhere who would tell candidates being urged by consultants in their own party to run against the leader, "Just Win Baby." Count me among the many Pelosi team members who have objected to that approach, telling her that people who support her don't want to have to give money to people who don't, or don't want to have to organize with people who don't defend her. I tell her all the time, "You have spoiled people—there will never be another party leader like you who ignores the abuse and spends money on other people instead of investing millions in responding to filth with positive ads." But she is unmoved. She believes we must all look at the bigger strategic picture: Votes are the currency of the realm. You cannot help people if you do not win, and you cannot win if you do not eat nails for breakfast, don a suit of armor, and go out into battle every day, knowing that the only preparation for combat is combat, so you'd better be prepared to take a punch and throw a punch for the children whose future you promised to protect. Nancy would say early on when running for Congress, "Political attacks can be awful— but they can't take my children from me so nothing they

think they could do to harm me would compare to that."
And that's just the way she is, often defining her service
this way: "My bosses, the voters, give me a job every
two years. They know that I'm not on a shift; I'm on a
mission."

In November 2016, the mission was clear: protect
the hard-fought gains of the Obama years and relin-
quish with joy the title of "highest-ranking woman in
American politics" to a female president. But fate—and
the Russians—intervened. Though she won the popular vote by over three million votes and came within
eighty thousand votes in three Midwestern states, Hillary
Rodham Clinton was not the president. Donald Trump
was—and through the shock and pain Nancy Pelosi
summoned her own advice: "Don't Agonize, Organize!"

9

Don't Agonize, Organize!

WHENEVER HER STAFF, FRIENDS, OR family reports about a nasty rumor or negative attack, Nancy Pelosi's response is practical: "We don't agonize—we organize!" Rather than internalize the attacks, or despair over bad news, channel pain into purpose.

Which leads us to November 2016, when the unthinkable happened: Donald Trump assumed the role of president-elect.

After a telephone call where he promised to work together on infrastructure, Nancy knew the stakes were highest for American's children, so she convened a phone meeting with volunteer stakeholders who had passed the Patient Protection and Affordable Care Act, and started making plans to save it. She knew she had to once again organize to "create her own environment" amid the crushing Clinton loss, the bitter transition from Obama to Trump, the self-described "United Republican Government" that was ready to repeal the PPACA once and for all, and a public challenge to her leadership.

Any one of these was agony to anyone without her political pain threshold, but she didn't flinch and kept to the mantra: "Don't agonize, organize."

Through dozens of calls with stakeholders, Nancy organized over Veterans Day weekend 2016, and the plans came into focus: Start a drumbeat across America to save the lifesaving care extended to millions of Americans.

As she told the Our Lives On The Line rally in the summer of 2017:

> Four days after the election we all got on the phone together: MoveOn, social media groups, we all got on the phone and understood one thing: whatever disagreements we might have or enthusiasms we do not share or do share, one thing was certain: we have to protect our care. And so right then and there people saw the urgency. When the marches came, the people saw their power. They knew their power. They marched for many reasons. One was to protect our care. And knowing and seeing the strength of their own actions, millions participated in town hall meetings and sit-ins or

called in to the offices of Republican members of Congress to tell their personal stories. Those stories were so inspirational, so eloquent. Nothing is more eloquent to a member of Congress than the voices of his or her own constituents. So that is why it is so important for my constituents not to necessarily call me to say thank you but to call their friends who live in Republican districts to call their elected officials.

That was the plan: begin with the coalition of patients, nurses, doctors, rural hospitals, and veterans' advocates, and widen the circles to include advocacy groups that helped pass the Patient Protection and Affordable Care Act in 2010 as well as—over time—the "resistance" groups that began in the weeks after the election.

Before Trump was inaugurated, Democrats had already held coast-to-coast rallies on Martin Luther King Jr. Day weekend, promising to save our care and protect patients with disabilities and diseases from a return to the bad old days where being a woman was a preexisting medical condition and patients were denied care or refused continuation of coverage once they reached a cap.

In addition to planning the health-care strategy, Nancy was negotiating the final legislation of the Obama administration during Congress's "Lame Duck" session— all the while running for and winning reelection as House Democratic leader with exactly the two-thirds vote she predicted she would receive from her caucus (68 percent) despite a breathless cable news campaign determined to undermine her leadership.

Despite the personal sadness of Hillary's loss, the mental burden of being personally vilified as being too old for her job, and the dark uncertainty of the CIA reports about Russia's active measures to interfere in the 2016 election, Nancy made a commitment to stay and, having done so, focused herself on what she did best: reviving a health-care coalition determined to provide a light of hope in the dark days of that angry winter.

Nancy began, as she often does, with a plan. She used the same playbook to stop the Patient Protection and Affordable Care Act repeal that she used to block George W. Bush's 2005 push to create private accounts under Social Security: organize the coalition of stakeholders to tell their own stories, educate people about the bad Republican plan to shred the safety net, compare their bad plan to the present, not to an alternative Democratic plan that people cannot visualize, and keep the pressure on for Republicans to reject their own plans as insufficient to meet the needs of the American people.

To begin, Nancy reminded everyone what had happened after the 2004 election. George W. Bush returned to Washington after his 2004 reelection victory claiming that he had a mandate to partially privatize Social Security. "I earned capital in the campaign, political capital," Bush said, "and I intend to spend it." Bush had a three-part plan: (1) Declare a crisis. (2) Tell people that a part of their money could be invested in the stock market. (3) Dare Democrats to come up with their own plans.

Bush (1) went to the State of the Union address and falsely said Social Security is "headed toward bankruptcy"; (2) reached out to seniors and to young people trying to convince them that, since the safety net wasn't going to be there for them in the long term, why not take their money now in the short term? and (3) with media allies, Bush tried to get Democrats to propose solutions that would bolster Social Security's finances while he was taking money out of the system! Nancy was not having any of it. She and Senate Democratic leader Harry Reid worked with President Lee Saunders of AFSCME and a coalition of labor and seniors' groups to turn out their members to community meetings. Wherever Bush went on the road to sell his plan, Democrats were on the trail with him, debunking his myths and refusing to put up any plan other than FDR in response.

It was not easy. Many seniors thought Social Security was in trouble. Young people polled said they thought they would not have money when it came time for their retirement. So the private funds seemed like a good idea. But Democrats asked the obvious question: "If you think it's going broke, why take more money out?" But there was still the risk of matter number 3.

Democrats have plans. Lots of plans. There may be more plans than Democrats, because some Democrats have multiple plans. However, they are a trap.

Conservative Democrats wanted to cut benefits. Liberal Democrats wanted to lift the caps (raise taxes). Nancy denied the crisis and refused all plans, saying they had to resist all the taunting from Republicans and enthusiasms from editorial boards—just explain why giving Enron and others who had crashed the energy markets a shot with your Social Security was a good idea. Picture that. When one member of Congress asked when Democrats would offer their own proposals, she replied, "Never. Is never good enough for you?"

The editorials were relentless. But so was Nancy. She never gave in.

She knew that plans would divide Democrats at a time when the party was unified. The coalition of students and seniors was holding meeting after meeting – and the strategy worked. "The first thing we had to do in 2005 was take the president's numbers down. Bush was 57 percent in early 2005, but his numbers came down to 38 in the fall, and that's when the retirements of congressional Republicans started to happen. Before his tour—and our tour—a majority of seniors thought private accounts were a good idea. By the fall, a majority opposed them."

At a spring 2005 meeting at the White House on an unrelated matter, President Bush noted that he had been to thirty cities on his tour. Nancy urged him to "double that," because everywhere he went, her people went, and her people were winning. Ultimately Bush caved, the plan collapsed, his numbers were down, House Republican retirements were up, and the Democrats swept to victory in 2006 in part on a promise to protect Social Security.

Keep in mind that while this was happening there was the constant complaint from Democrats who wanted their plans and Very Serious People in Washington who recoiled at the notion that Nancy was taking down Bush's plan the way aspirin companies compete with each other. They wanted compromise—which to them of course meant that poor seniors were going to sacrifice. Not a chance. Nancy withstood the slings and arrows of the chattering class that was convinced she was wrong. But she won.

In 2017, Nancy had a plan, and, as had been the case in 2005, she had plenty of doubters. Rather than having Democrats bet against ourselves by begging Trump to stop parts of the repeal, Nancy bet on the Patient Protection and Affordable Care Act and the public's desire to expand rather than shred the safety net. She refused to offer an alternative, saying the law *is* the alternative and that it was a mistake to confuse people with an alternative they would not understand. She had learned through the selling of the Patient Protection and Affordable Care Act that people are not sold on hypothetical benefits and that that Republican "fog of controversy" can always cloud new plans. Why fall into that trap again? The stakes were just too high. Instead the focus was on protecting what we have now, a promise to collect the list of fixes to work on after defeating the Trump repeal that would strip affordable care from millions and deny patient protections to millions more, and maintaining the focus on Trump's repeal and sabotage and how bad it would be for patients.

In those early days before the inauguration, the raw pain felt by women who believed that Hillary Rodham Clinton was the most qualified candidate for president and had lost to a far inferior man was intense and was channeled into activism. Tens of thousands of people joined the #OurFirstStand weekend of action.

In San Francisco, over three thousand people showed up to voice their support. They were rapt with attention as they listened to the stories that were told about how people would be affected, whether it was a person with a preexisting condition, somebody affected by lifetime caps on personal medical care for disease or disability, or those talking about their children being able to stay on their plans until age twenty-six. People all over the country were supportive of not repealing the Patient Protection and Affordable Care Act until we have something to replace it with, and Nancy was not going to offer that until she had defeated repeal. As she said often those early days of resistance to Trump, "It's one thing for us to try to sell it to the American people, it's another thing for the Republicans to take it away."

So Nancy set out to tell people what Trump was taking away: patient protections for 130 million Americans with preexisting medical conditions and access to care for over 20 million Americans who had been added to the rolls. In addition, there were costs of "uncompensated care" to hospitals, because hospitals must treat people who come, and if it isn't paid for, the hospitals have to close. This was already happening to rural hospitals in states where Republicans had not expanded Medicaid, and repeal would make matters worse. The strategy was to make this about the health of each person in the country and ask constituents to tell their own stories.

The biggest difference between 2010 and 2017 was truth, what Nancy called "the living truth that people have experienced in their lives." Rather than be scared by what might happen, people could say what had happened and what more they needed to make their care better. Nancy said, "The truth is on our side, and it is told by the people themselves."

Nancy met with everyone from social media organizers to the groups that helped pass the Patient Protection and Affordable Care Act. They ranged from people with disabilities to mental illness advocates to seniors, children, hospitals, and faith-based organizations. For the first time, the polls said that approval for the health-care law was higher than disapproval. People knew what it meant to their lives, so they were willing to defend it even as they sought expansions of care. Seventy percent of the people polled said they didn't want it to be repealed without a replacement.

Nancy reminded everyone of the stakes: "If you're a child and you're born with a preexisting condition, it's your life and your family. You want to go get a job? You apply for a job, your prospective employer finds out that your wife might have breast cancer, that's going to hike up the insurance rates for the whole firm? See you later. Now that's what we were living with before." She shared that when she went to get health insurance, "They told me, 'You're poor risk, you've had five children.' I said, 'I've had five children, I'm stronger than you are.' What do you mean, 'poor risk'?" Everyone had a story. Our mission was to get the stories told.

The next weekend, on inauguration weekend, millions came out to protest and protect in crowds dwarfing the already unusually small Trump inaugural parade with a powerful international Women's March. On the inauguration podium, Nancy wore a Protect Our Care button to let everyone know the battle lines were drawn. The next day, as Nancy joined Women's March Bay Area walking down San Francisco's Market Street in the rain surrounded by deeply dispirited volunteers who had worked on her House races and Hillary's campaign, she did not miss a step. She encouraged those assembled to "volunteer and vote" and "protect our care." And, loudest of the many chants, "Don't agonize, organize!"

And so it began. Born of sadness and recriminations, misogyny from the White House sometimes echoed by the left, and the chaos of some who simply could not stop relitigating the 2016 Democratic presidential primary or would not stop chasing the fickle Trump-Obama voters at the expense of the party faithful. The grassroots were restless and distrustful and some flat-out refused to welcome in the new volunteers, most of whom were women and many of whom were people with preexisting medical conditions or family health problems. The group dynamics were precarious at best. But Nancy just kept convening, cajoling, listening, and taking in every single detail about the Republican House members and senators who needed to vote down the health-care repeal their new president had promised.

With the same precision with which Nancy promised to "push through the gate" to pass health care in 2010, she focused relentlessly on every point of advocacy. Every week she met on the phone and in the communities with health-care advocates and listened to their ideas about what messages were resonating, who was willing to make calls, and who could provide volunteers. Every bit of data went into her mental encyclopedia and resulted in more concentric circles of people whipping the votes. Everyone who wanted to participate played a part in making repeal and sabotage "too hot to handle." Telling those personal stories and giving the microphone to the patients themselves was the key to saving Social Security in 2005, and it was the same in 2017. The difference was in the technology, because with social media the "protect our care" message went farther and faster. She knew that the Republicans would attack anyone attacking repeal, so she insisted on a support group of people to lift up the patients and their families so that when the attacks came, people would have online support from other people sharing their own stories and defending the advocates with love.

Nancy had four main points hammered in over and over: Trump would raise out-of-pocket costs, hurt people between the ages of forty and sixty-five, destroy the Medicare guarantee, and strip away coverage from 24 million people.

In March 2017, there was a tension in the coalition. A poll of Trump-Obama voters revealed that Democrats could save Social Security disability benefits and Medicare from Republican repeals and budget raids—but not Medicaid. Either people said they don't know anyone on Medicaid or their states had not passed Medicaid expansion (and had the highest risk of health problems and of rural hospital closures). The pollsters were trying to convince Democratic lawmakers to drop Medicaid from the messaging in order to reach those Trump-Obama voters.

Nancy was not convinced. She recognized that people didn't see Medicaid having a connection to their lives so she worked with a coalition of patients determined to change that. Veterans, people with disabilities, and children with complex medical conditions told her that they would step up and became the faces of Medicaid—and Nancy lifted them up into the Protect Our Care messaging despite the polling that suggested otherwise. The VoteVets group of post-9/11 veterans was intrepid. They had a national network of people talking about how 1.79 million veterans were on Medicaid after serving this country and should not be kicked off. Seniors became active in the coalition: Over 60 percent of the funds for long-term health care for seniors are paid for from Medicaid. They are middle-income seniors in nursing homes or at home receiving care. Parents of children with disabilities—even families that have employer-based insurance—need Medicaid for added coverage or to cover the attendants and educators in schools or home care.

Nancy took in information unfiltered from people on the front lines, like the kids with complex medical conditions who renamed themselves the Little Lobbyists who became fixtures in the field and at her press conferences and their teachers who talked about the educators of disabled kids funded by Medicaid.

Their parents gave them a voice, and the kids were terrific faces of care.

Their parents talked about the catastrophic effects of Trump's proposed Medicaid cuts. Without the Patient Protection and Affordable Care Act, most of these kids would have exceeded their lifetime cap before ever coming home from the hospital and would have been uninsurable. As Nancy often said, "The Little Lobbyists have made all the difference in the world. You do not want to stand in between one of these moms and the good health care of her child." According to Little Lobbyists cofounder Elena Hung, whose daughter Xiomara has chronic lung and kidney disease, nearly three hundred families in forty-seven states have shared their personal stories with Congress.

The health-care advocates and disability rights groups found common cause with the gun-violence-prevention advocates. Survivors Empowered cofounders Lonnie and Sandy Phillips, whose daughter Jessi was murdered at the Aurora, Colorado, movie theater massacre, educated the coalition on the health impact: once your child is killed, you have a preexisting medical condition. Advocates from Everytown, Newtown Action Alliance, Moms Demand Action, Brady, Parkland survivors (students organized as March for Our Lives and parents including Manuel Oliver and Fred Guttenberg), and the Gabby Giffords Law Center were instrumental in lifting up the message that gun violence victims and survivors are patients for life. Making gun violence a public health issue gave people a deeper understanding of the consequences of the nearly 40,000 people who perished in gun-related deaths in the United States in 2018.

One thing that came out of all the storytelling and all the organizing was unity around the principle that health care is a right for all and not a privilege just for the few. Second, Medicaid is important to every family in America, whether they know it yet or not. And third, there were ideas on how to improve and update the Patient Protection and Affordable Care Act, a pillar of economic and health security with Social Security, Medicare, and Medicaid.

By summer 2017, health care was top of mind for most voters. Nancy spearheaded calls with key stakeholders and activists from across the country once, sometimes even twice a week. She joined the grassroots advocates at hundreds of press conferences, rallies, and rapid response events.

No event was too small or too big for her. At one point in June 2017, Nancy showed up ten minutes prior to the start of a rally outside the Capitol. Activists from MoveOn, Social Security Works, and Center for Popular Democracy could be seen from a distance carrying a podium, speakers, mics, signage, and water for participants to keep cool during the hot summer. The rally went from having only Pelosi and her staff to over sixty folks in a matter of minutes.

On a warm June evening Nancy addressed the Protect Our Care coalition on the Capitol lawn along with stalwarts from VoteVets, Little Lobbyists, Save Our Care, MoveOn, Center for Popular Democracy, Ady Barkan's Be A Hero, ADAPT, Planned Parenthood, People for the American Way, AFL-CIO, AFSCME, SEIU, AFT, the HUB Project, and others who had been holding constant vigils.

Watching and live-tweeting from home, I heard her rev up the troops, then start to talk about Republican Senator John McCain, who was undergoing cancer treatment. I left her a message—we of course want to wish people well, but why was she singling him out for praise and prayers when we had other senators we needed too? Democrat Mazie Hirono of Hawaii left her cancer treatments to come back and vote in the Senate—what about Mazie? Nancy returned my call and responded to what she described as my "stern" voice mail message asking me

to trust her and to just keep calm. Well, she knew or sus-
pected something the rest of America didn't, because the
following day, Senator McCain walked onto the Senate
floor for the repeal vote of his 2008 presidential opponent Barack Obama's key accomplishment, huddled
with some colleagues, then raised his arm and lowered
the boom: thumbs down to repeal.

When I told this story to former Congressman George
Miller, he laughed and said, "See? Nancy knew Mazie
Hirono would be fine with singling out McCain because
all the senators knew he was the swing vote. Nancy knows
where she can go with people. You didn't have the whole
story—she did. Nobody has the whole story—except her
and she's not telling."

What we see as activists and what she sees as a leader
weaving and whipping her votes are vastly different in
scope. The truth was, in 2010 when they were whipping their final votes to pass the bill, Nancy looked out
on the Capitol steps and saw tea party protesters with
effigies of herself and President Obama. No air cover or
ground cover for her side. But in 2017, she had made her
own media and built her own ground game. She was not
going into battle exposed or waiting for someone else to
come to the rescue. While both times there were many
groups engaged in the fight, the fact was that in 2010 the
voices of the patients were drowned out in the "fog of
controversy." She was not going to let that happen again.
And so this time out on the Capitol steps she looked out

to see her grassroots allies. And, confident that she had come to her own rescue, she picked up the phone and called Senator McCain.

Once again, Nancy Pelosi's wisdom prevailed: don't agonize, organize!

On another occasion during the evening of July 29, 2017, Nancy joined over six hundred passionate activists as the guest speaker for the Our Lives on the Line rally to protect health care. The next morning, she held an hour-long grassroots call on the importance of owning the messaging during the month of August and ensuring the American people held House Republicans responsible for voting to take away their health care, all while on her way to depart for an overseas congressional delegation.

The fight continued, and the Republicans offered a new repeal bill, which meant the return to Capitol Hill by the Little Lobbyists. Nancy had just kicked off a press conference honoring the "VIPs—very important people: our children, our future, the Little Lobbyists." Armed with these stories, we will finally put a stake in the heart of this monstrous bill. . . . These families and families like them have been with us from the start. They helped us push open the gate when there was an obstacle to passing the Patient Protection and Affordable Care Act. Here now, again to protect our care."

A reporter interjected: "Well, you've convinced the Leader of the Senate Mitch McConnell because he said there will be no vote on the Graham-Cassidy bill."

Everybody cheered.

The victory was sweet, but only temporary. Unfortunately the Republican tax bill passed the Senate, and the Republicans had a keg party in the White House Rose Garden.

In that moment, Nancy and the coalition did not waver, but took up the lesson: "Don't agonize, organize."

People shared the photos of the Republicans laughing at the keg party to celebrate undermining a pillar of financial and health security in our country—and redoubled efforts to mobilize.

So successful was the strategy that by the fall of 2018, every Republican candidate was claiming to protect pre-existing medical conditions benefits—even though all of them refused to call on President Trump to stop his lawsuit against the Patient Protection and Affordable Care Act.

Taken together, the calls and marches and sit-ins and educational hearings all coalesced in ten thousand grassroots events to protect health care. That in turn galvanized Get Out the Vote efforts.

By election night 2018, a new majority had been swept into power with a mandate to save health care. The same health care bill that lost the House in 2010 was the key to winning it back for the people in 2018. As for the Rose Garden keg party celebration of throwing people off health care? Most of the congresspeople present had been voted out.

Nancy said in 2010 when asked about four different

versions of the Patient Protection and Affordable Care Act: "We have to pass the bill so you can find out what's in it away from the fog of controversy."

Well, the Republicans created and maintained the "fog of controversy" with considerable help from the special interests opposed to change. Over 130 million American families have patient protections and lifesaving health care.

And as Nancy predicted, people found out what was in the bill—patient protections adopted from the Patients' Bill of Rights and the affordable care provided in states that established exchanges and expanded Medicaid. They wanted to protect and expand, rather than destroy, affordable care.

No one was fooled. The Trump tax bill took money from the middle class to fund a tax break for the most wealthy while stealing from the American safety net designed to lift up the most poor and vulnerable. Once again, Nancy did not waste a single second. Traveling from city to city across the country, Pelosi joined the Tax March for "teach-ins" about the harmful impact then-Speaker Paul Ryan's tax scam would consequently have on Medicare, Medicaid, and Social Security. From Houston to Orlando, from Boston to Chicago and San Francisco, Nancy joined hundreds of local activists and families concerned about the monstrosity of the bill.

The on-the-ground organizing and our coalition got a boost from what we call the "tweet heard around the world." Paul Ryan, on a Saturday midafternoon in

February, outrageously tweeted—then deleted—that a secretary from Pennsylvania was pleasantly surprised by receiving "a $1.50 increase" in her paycheck, all while the press was reporting that the Koch brothers were on track to receive almost a billion a year from the tax scam. Team Pelosi wasted no time capitalizing on the gross admission, tweeting about it and generating over 23,000 retweets and dozens of mentions in key articles, mobilizing groups, and sharing social media messaging.

The incident also laid bare something that had been building for a while: The public was disenchanted with Republican claims to be helping patients and saw instead that Republican lawmakers were only helping themselves and their donors.

First of all, the Republicans had voted to repeal the Patient Protection and Affordable Care Act over fifty times when Barack Obama was president, so one would think they would have a replacement plan at the ready. After all, "proper preparation prevents poor performance." Right? Wrong. There was no plan, and it showed. Second, most Americans polled in 2018 believed the economy was improving but had real concerns about their own personal finances. That has actually been true since Barack Obama was president, and was why, when Democrats tried to run on an improved economy, people were still unconvinced that the rising tide had lifted their personal boats. What people did see was the wealthy getting wealthier for the past two decades and wealthy political donors having their way in Washington. The issue of corruption really rankled people. It wasn't simply the "pox on all houses," "all politicians are corrupt" notion; it was a deeper sense that while some people will always do better than others, Washington and everyone in it is subject to temptation; there are deep concerns about the role of big money in all of politics. Democrats responded with a debate about the intraparty role of corporate money in politics and the need to forcefully separate contributions from policy-making. Some are refusing corporate PAC donations altogether; most eschewed contributions that conflict with their governing platform. The "No NRA" money pledge was one example of a campaign to forcefully refuse campaign contributions from the gun lobby that was stopping bipartisan background checks and other life-saving measures. Congressional Republicans, on the other hand, felt no such restrictions. Working with groups such as End Citizens United, Common Cause, and Public Citizen, Nancy built support for proposals by John Sarbanes to reduce the role of special interest money in Congress and by Alabama congresswoman Terri Sewell to restore and expand the Voting Rights Act. That Paul Ryan tweet confirmed their worst fears, which is why it resonated so hard. That $1.50 raise wasn't trickle down, it was barely a spray mist, and the reaction was swift and fierce.

Yes, it is true that politicians of both parties have bragged about a $300 stimulus or a $2,000 tax credit. But $1.50 a paycheck compared to billions for the companies? Nancy got enormous outrage from the right for calling that crumbs from the banquet table, but as it turns out she was correct, and the public agreed with her. Something fundamental within the economy had changed, and voters were looking to make someone pay.

But would it be all politicians or just Republicans?

This is where Trump came in. Many people voted for Trump to "shake up the system" while giving his sexist and racist comments a pass. The reports on where Trump had won early described communities of wage stagnation from 2004 to 2014, jobs lost to globalization or automation, and so-called "white distress"—a combination of reduced white participation in the workplace and either outright racism or expressed concern about white Americans' declining dominance together with the rising status of African Americans, Latinos, and immigrants in communities of color.[19]

As in 2006, Nancy had promised that the first bill in the new Congress would address open government. In 2006 the bill was introduced by then-Senator Barack Obama; in 2018; the House Democrats ran on a For the People agenda to reduce the role of dark money in politics, publicly finance campaigns, disclose donors, and reform ethics rules. It was overwhelmingly popular on the campaign trail.

Having spent her career empowering people to answer a call to service, take a political risk, and build coalitions for change, Nancy knows that political disparities begin

19 "The United States of Trump," NBC News, June 20, 2016, https://shortyawards.com/9th/nbc-news-united-states-of-trump

in the voting booth. All other rights flow from voting rights, so we must ensure that more people are registered, voting, volunteering, and serving in public life. She knows that this path has been blocked by voter suppression and negative attack ads funded by dark special-interest money and funneled through groups like ALEC and the Koch organizations. So she added a voting rights component to the message, and voters concerned about their health care saw Republicans try to take it away, funded by wealthy secret donors who got far more out of the tax scam than regular people did. The whole operation was led by the person who lied to them about protecting their care and lived in a gilded way while they continued to struggle. Election advantage and policy opportunity went to the Democrats. The interlocking messages of health care and fighting corruption and putting a check on Trump boosted Democratic turnout.

She took nothing for granted. Traveling the country, raising nearly a quarter of a billion dollars, and tending to the grassroots "down to every blade of grass," Nancy was a woman on a mission. Rather than campaign for herself, she opened up a campaign headquarters in San Francisco with the local Democratic Party. Together with local party leaders David Campos and Sophie Maxwell, she recruited over 2,500 volunteers to call and text over a million voters in twenty congressional districts. With daily organizing fortified by the Blue Wave Cafe, everyone had a role in building the victory. Sixteen of those races brought new faces to Congress—in eleven instances, the

Red to Blue SF team "yes" votes were within the margin of victory.

Every night the theme was the same: "protect our care" and win "for the people."

The lesson: the fog of controversy will always be there, so you must create your own environment and have people tell their own stories to make change and to guard human rights. And on matters as deeply personal as health care, it is vital to have the organizer's vision: put aside the old ways of telling other people's stories and instead listen to them tell themselves.

Stories about health care; stories about immigration; stories about climate justice; stories about violence against women (an outpouring of which followed the nomination hearings of Supreme Court Justice Brett Kavanaugh and the riveting testimony of Dr. Christine Blasey Ford, who accused him of assaulting her when they were teenagers); stories about institutionalized racism and inequality all empowered people to take personal responsibility to make the future better and to make their own media narratives rather than be drowned out or marginalized. From her years on the House Appropriations Committee, Nancy adopted the phrase "the plural of anecdote is not data." One story, no matter how powerful, does not tell the whole story. We need more voices, more data points, more science, and more peer review to make decisions rooted in facts and truth. And conversely, we cannot let one story or mischaracterization derail our progress.

Winning any issue requires the same steady resolve. Never leaving constituencies behind, Nancy focused the official and campaign message on working for the people. And won. But before she could savor the Democrats' victory, there was one more race to win: reclaiming the Speaker's gavel.

The elements were not complicated—it was simply a matter of methodically counting and weaving votes one person and one story at a time. The process was arduous because everyone came in with lots of ideas about how to organize the new Congress, and the new people who had never served were suddenly coming into a new job, with new responsibilities, and new visibility on their choices for Speaker.

The vast majority of votes were there from the start. There were two unknowns: people who were pledging to vote no under any circumstances and people whose minds could be changed.

The coalition that had worked to save health care and mobilize for the elections mobilized again. Every day there were letters from friends and allies—labor unions, women's groups, individual supporters, former colleagues, and the vast network of members already setting up their work in the majority and ready to either have a race between candidates or move on.

Because her opposition's theory was to push her out and then start over, many who entered Congress undecided about the Speaker's race were unimpressed. Having won their own races by competing, they did not see the value of forcing someone out as opposed to posting an opponent.

Others had genuine concerns about the direction of the caucus and wanted to be sure their voices would be heard in terms of bills they wanted prioritized, open lines of communications, and structural reforms to internal proceedings so that more people could run for caucus positions. Reality check: 7 percent of voters in battleground districts said that the speaker vote or Nancy Pelosi herself was one of the top two issues in their vote for Congress, according to a *Washington Post*/Schar School poll. Of those 7 percent, 88 percent supported Republican candidates, while 12 percent supported Democrats. So we are talking about 12 percent of 7 percent of the vote in targeted districts. After 137,000 negative ads, Nancy was hardly the bogeywoman painted by some who first said she could not lead, then said she could not win, and now said she could not win again. As it happens, voters cared much more about health care and their personal economy than they did who was Speaker of the House. It was essentially coming down to the people who had said no on the campaign trail and kept their word, the people who were undecided who had to make a decision, and the people who gave voice to opposition but were willing to change their minds. There was a fog of controversy and there were some hard no votes. Full stop. But there was enough room for conversation and persuasion to lock in the 218 votes.

First of all, Democrats had won, which took away the "Nancy cannot win" argument. Second, many people were elected and reelected because a wave of women voters came out to the polls. To then turn around and fire the woman leader without a competition seemed a bad fit. Third, most supporters highlighted Nancy's qualifications as tough in the trenches, as principled in her consistent votes for the Democratic coalition, and as proactive in anticipating and executing strategy. Nancy made it clear that being Speaker was not something she deserved—it was a job she had earned and was ready to fight for.[20]

In the race for the gavel, people who had worked in the tough fights with Nancy from the AFL-CIO to key women's groups vouched for her stamina and integrity. AFSCME President Lee Saunders wrote in a letter that Pelosi "consistently stood with the hard-working men and women" of his union, while teachers union president Randi Weingarten declared "When you look at the situation right now, today, there is no candidate that is better than Nancy Pelosi." Former Pelosi staffer, Planned Parenthood president, and SuperMajority cofounder Cecile Richards said: "I've actually been there in the trenches with her. To me, she is unequivocally the most principled leader that I've ever had the chance to work with in Congress." Over and over the message was clear:

---

20   Mike DeBonis and Elise Viebeck, "Pelosi moves aggressively to snuff out challenge to her bid for House speaker," *The Washington Post,* November 12, 2018, https://www.washingtonpost.com/powerpost/pelosi-moves-aggressively-to-snuff-out-challenge-to-her-bid-for-house-speaker/2018/11/12/49d008b8-e6b3-11e8-bbdb-72fdbf9d4fed_story.html

the troubled times called for experience in the moment and mentoring for the future. With her commitment to an eight-year speakership term limit—same as a president's—the race was clinched. After weeks of being a great listener, Nancy was poised to be a great Speaker.

10

Know Your Power (Reprise)

IN DISCUSSIONS WITH PERSONS FOR this book, the recurring theme was the difference between Nancy Pelosi as the first and the second woman speaker.

Whatever people throw at her, she can take; whatever internal family dramas, she sees the bigger picture; whatever personal invective in strongly sexist terms, she doesn't get rattled and stays focused on her plan. No matter the competing strands of an internationally diverse caucus, the weaver works at her loom, listening and responding, counting her votes and her blessings, seeing opportunity where others see (or try to create) chaos. She often quotes Thomas Paine, the philosopher, author, and Founder who said "the times have found us."

And though she has for decades pledged "to live up to the vision of our founders, the sacrifice of our men and women in uniform, and the aspirations of our children," the times feel more urgent.

As one close family friend put it, "I'm more proud now because of the dignity, purpose, and even-handedness she is bringing the second time. She seems liberated." Another agreed: "No matter how many times people complain that they want things to be done faster or differently or want to divide Democrats so that they can say all politics is broken as opposed to the parts that actually are broken and Democrats are fixing, she stays on course." Another said, "The first time she won she said 'look I have my own flag.'" Now she is awed but not starstruck by the job, wearing a mace pin symbolizing the Speaker's office and talking about the "awesome" power and responsibility of the office.

There will be passion. There will be the growing pains of a new majority and 235 powerful people learning to work together and serve together, but that's the job. "As the opening session began, she took some tough shots and was able to let that play out," says former congressman George Miller. "She didn't think about what she needed as an individual—she was thinking about what all 235 people needed." Over and over she would tell the members: "Our diversity is our strength; our unity is our power."

When Democrats lost the House in 2010, there were many angry people looking to push Nancy out too. As a family, we met and said, as we had the very first time she ran: "Look, we are for you. If you want to run for leader again, we are with you, and if not, our children will be lucky to have more time with their Mimi, and you and Dad have certainly earned a peaceful retirement." As a daughter I'm always ambivalent—selfish for my own children and the time they could have with their grandmother. But as an activist I'm glad she didn't give up and kept weaving a more inclusive and progressive agenda.

Once she and the House Democratic Caucus made the decision for her to stay on, I asked the staff for a constituent service. On her last day as Speaker in 2010, after Nancy gaveled in the repeal of the Don't Ask, Don't Tell military discrimination policy, I asked for the flags flown above the Capitol and promised myself they would fly again when Democrats retook the House. It took longer than I thought, and the journey was more painful for the country than I'd hoped, but because she never gave up, and the people she serves never gave up, on January 3, 2019, when Nancy Pelosi took the gavel surrounded by children to became the second woman Speaker of the House, those flags flew over the United States Capitol again.

And under those flags, she began the 116th Congress by weaving this part of the tapestry while remaining acutely aware of the dangers to democracy and the fragility of the national safety net. She weaves this tapestry with the most diverse Congress in history protecting the American dream of human progress, civil rights, health care, respect, and dignity for the most vulnerable among us; preserving the environment against the climate crisis, and strengthening the bonds between people, in communities, and among nations. In June 2019, when *MetroWeekly* asked her if being in politics ever changed her personally, Nancy responded:

> Nothing to me is more of an honor than to walk on the floor of the House each legislative day, sent by the people of San Francisco. So while my colleagues have given me great honors and I thank them for that and I feel blessed by them, to speak for the people of San Francisco is the biggest honor of all. Having said that, I am grateful to my colleagues for giving me the opportunity I've had to lead, to listen, and to build consensus within our caucus.

Nancy is in her prime as a mentor, leader, and weaver, in it to show women that we should not be pushed around—that we have to stand our ground, know what we believe, and fight for it.

Although politics are quite raw and raucous, and it will take years to heal the pain and collective trauma of the Trump era, the north star is a shared dedication to what America can be and what we have in ourselves to give.

As she often asks:

> What is America? America is our Constitution, the beauty of it: a system of checks and balances,

separation of power, separate branches of government—coequal as a check on each other, the freedom to continue in our Constitution, and to thank God—they put in to amend our Constitution. What is America? America is our beautiful land, from sea to shining sea. What is America? It's who we are. Unless you are born to be a Native American, which is a blessing to you and to all who know you, and to our country, but by and large we are a nation of immigrants. America is a great country and a shared set of values about how we care about people and the sense of community that drives us into public service.[21]

Nancy is weaving big plans into the fabric of history, honoring that vision of America, the vows of our founders, the sacrifice of our women and men in uniform, and the aspirations of our children.

---

21   September 26, 2019 address to NARAL.

Afterword

As we went to print, the Speaker was in the process of opening an impeachment inquiry into the president of the United States. A whistleblower complaint of "urgent concern"—under the law Nancy helped write and pass—reported a presidential threat to the president of Ukraine seeking a favor of opposition research on former vice president Joe Biden in exchange for the release of congressionally approved funds. The allegations shook the Capitol—and were borne out in a White House memo of notes and recollections regarding the call and a spoken confession from the president himself. The years-long calls for impeachment regarding various misdeeds crescendoed with this very sobering potential national security breach. Over the weekend of September 21, 2019, Nancy decided to support an inquiry. She called member after member, weaving (not whipping) this seminal vote of conscience for the Congress. This was not an easy decision, but rather a somber and prayerful time. Members who had not run for Congress to impeach a president saw this brazen admission of a serious breach of constitutional duties as evidence enough to begin an inquiry.

By Monday, the dam was breaking as more members declared that Congress had to open an impeachment inquiry to uphold their oath to support and defend the Constitution, putting duty to country first. By Tuesday, it was time to make the formal announcement. Civil rights icon John Lewis, representative of Georgia and the "conscience of the Congress," made a rousing floor speech summoning America to the moment: "We cannot delay. We must not wait. Now is the time to act. I have been patient while we tried every other path and used every other tool. We will never find the truth unless we use the power given to the House of Representatives and the House alone to begin an official investigation as dictated by the Constitution. The future of our democracy is at stake."

He continued: "I believe, I truly believe, the time to begin impeachment proceedings against this president has come. To delay, or to do otherwise, would betray the foundation of our democracy."

A few hours later, with the solemnity required, Nancy herself addressed the nation.

"The times have found us," she said, quoting Thomas Paine, who delivered those somber remarks during the darkest times of the American Revolution. "The times found them to fight for and establish our democracy. The times have found us today," she said, to fight for our nation's democracy and deliver on our promise to help working families across our country.

The next morning Trump tried to bargain away her resolve, to no avail—"tell your people to obey the law," Nancy told the president on an early morning call. She would not be moved. The next day, he had House Republicans try to offer a motion of disapproval of Nancy as Speaker and of the impeachment inquiry. The motion was tabled. Seated in the gallery, I could feel the momentum literally shift as a majority of the House backed her up. No angry tweets or bilious words or scurrilous motions would keep her from her path. Drawing upon a lifetime of lessons, she will direct the impeachment inquiry the Nancy Pelosi way: knowing her power and responsibility under the Constitution, being properly prepared, speaking from her own authentic self, confident at the table, building strategic alliances, showing her why, weaving consensus, withstanding the criticism from right and left, being determined to organize, not agonize through the fog of controversy, and when the time comes, using her power for the people.

Address by Representative Nancy Pelosi of California
September 24, 2019

Good afternoon. Last Tuesday, we observed the anniversary of the adoption of the Constitution on

September 17th. Sadly, on that day, the Intelligence Community Inspector General formally notified the Congress that the administration was forbidding him from turning over a whistleblower complaint on Constitution Day.

This is a violation of the law. Shortly thereafter, press reports began to break of a phone call by the President of the United States, calling upon a foreign power to intervene in his election. This is a breach of his constitutional responsibilities.

The facts are these. The Intelligence Community Inspector General, who was appointed by President Trump, determined that the complaint is both of urgent concern and credible, and its disclosure, he went on to say, relates to one of the most significant and important of the Director of National Intelligence's responsibility to the American people.

On Thursday, the Inspector General testified before the House Intelligence Committee, stating that the Acting Director of National Intelligence barred him from disclosing the whistleblower complaint. This is a violation of law.

The law is unequivocal. The DNI staff, it says the DNI—DNI, Director of National Intelligence— shall provide Congress the full whistleblower complaint. For more than twenty-five years, I've served on the Intelligence Committee as a member—as the ranking member as part of the Gang of Four even before I was in the leadership.

I was there when we created the Office of the Director of National Intelligence. That did not exist before 2004. I was there even earlier in the '90s when we wrote the whistleblower laws and continue to write them to improve them to ensure the security of our intelligence and the safety of our whistleblowers.

I know what their purpose was and we proceeded with balance and caution as we wrote the laws. I can say with authority that the Trump administration's actions undermine both our national security and our intelligence and our protections of the whistleblowers, more than both.

This Thursday, the Acting DNI will appear before the House Intelligence Committee. At that time, he must turn over the whistleblower's full complaint to the Committee. He will have to choose whether to break the law or honor his responsibility to the Constitution.

On the final day of the Constitutional Convention in 1787, when our Constitution was adopted, Americans gathered on the steps of Independence Hall to await the news of a government our founders had crafted. They asked Benjamin Franklin, "What do we have, a republic or a monarchy?" Franklin replied, "A republic, if you can keep it." Our responsibility is to keep it. Our public endures because of the wisdom of our Constitution enshrined in three coequal branches of government serving as checks and balances on each other.

The actions taken to date by the President have seriously violated the Constitution, especially when the President says Article II says "I can do whatever I want." For the past several months, we have been investigating in our committees and litigating in the courts so the House can gather all of the relevant facts and consider whether to exercise its full Article I powers, including a constitutional power of the utmost gravity, approval of Articles of Impeachment.

And this week, the President has admitted to asking the President of Ukraine to take actions which would benefit him politically. The action of the Trump—the actions of the Trump presidency revealed a dishonorable fact of the President's betrayal of his oath of office, betrayal of our national, and betrayal of the integrity of our elections.

Therefore today, I'm announcing the House of Representatives moving forward with an official impeachment inquiry. I am directing our six committees to proceed with their investigations under that umbrella of impeachment inquiry.

The President must be held accountable. No one is above the law. Getting back to our founders, in the darkest days of the American Revolution, Thomas Paine wrote that times have found us, that times found them to fight for and establish our democracy. The times have found us today.

Not to place ourselves in the same category of greatness as our founders but to place us in the urgency of protecting and defending our Constitution from all enemies, foreign and domestic. In the words of Ben Franklin, to keep our republic.

I thank our Chairmen, Chairman Nadler of Judiciary, Chairman Schiff of Intelligence, Chairman Engel, Foreign Affairs, Chairman Cummings, Oversight. And Chairman Cummings, I've been in touch with constantly, he's a master of so much, but including Inspectors General and whistleblowers.

Congressman Richie Neal of the Ways and Means Committee, Congresswoman Maxine Waters of the Financial Services Committee, and I commend all of our members, our colleagues for their thoughtful, thoughtful approach to all of this, for their careful statements. God bless them and God bless America. Thank you all.

Acknowledgments

First, last, and always thank you Nancy Pelosi for your leadership with a heart full of love for your country and your family. You inspire me every day as a mom, a mentor, and a model for women and girls.

Thank you Pop, who walked into an amazing adventure years ago at that Georgetown summer school class—and have embodied dedication and patience as a friend, husband, father, and grandfather. Thank you to Nancy Corinne, Jeff, Alexander, and Madeleine Prowda; Jacqueline, Michael, Liam, Sean, and Ryan Kenneally; Paul Pelosi Jr.; and Alexandra, Michiel, Paul, and Thomas Vos; Kelly and Phil; Octavio, Peter, and Bella Kaufman. Thank you for the insights, Uncle Tommy D'Alesandro, Hon. George Miller, Hon. Anna Eshoo, Hon. Tim Roemer, Rita Meyer, Mary and Steven Swig.

Thank you everyone on Team Pelosi organizing from the first house meeting to the latest social media warriors tweetstorm—your hard work and dedication has helped elect an extraordinary leader and a generation of Democratic majority makers to advance progress in the lives of the American people. Thank you to the Speaker's Congressional staff, especially Drew Hammill, Taylor Griffin, Julio Obscura, and Dan Bernal, and the campaign team led by Jorge Aguilar, for the photos and stories.

To all the volunteers who phoned, walked, knocked, texted, and turned your personal stories into political action, thank you for picking up the mantra "don't agonize, organize!" You marched with communities and coalitions and built over 10,000 grassroots events to protect our health care, change the world, and turn passion into action every day. Thank you to every member or partner of ACLU, ADAPT, AFGE, AFL-CIO, AFSCME, AFT, Alliance for Retired Americans, America's Voice, Americans for Tax Fairness, APALA, Association of Flight Attendants-CWA, Be a Hero, Bend the Arc, Brady Campaign, California Democratic Party, Center for Popular Democracy, CHIRLA, Common Cause, Daily Kos, Demand Progress, Democratic Coalition, Democratic National Committee, Doctors for America, End Citizens United, Equality Florida, Fight For 15, Giffords Law Center, Health Care for America Now, Housing Works, Hub Project, Human Rights Campaign, Indivisible chapters, League of Conservation

Voters, Little Lobbyists, Leadership Conference on Civil Rights, Mamás Con Poder, March for Our Lives, March Forward, Mi Famila Vota, Moms Demand Action/ Everytown, Moms In Charge, MomsRising, MoveOn, NARAL, National Action Network, National Union of Healthcare Workers, NEA, Newtown's Action Alliance, NextGen America, NoNRA, Not One Penny, NOW, NWPC, Occupy Democrats, Oil Change International, Orange Ribbons for Jaime, Organizing for America, Our Lives on the Line, People for the American Way, Patriotic Millionaires, People's Action, People Demanding Action, Planned Parenthood, Poor People's Campaign, Progress Now, Protect Our Care, Public Citizen, Rapid Resist, San Francisco Democratic Party, San Francisco Labor Council, SEIU, Sierra Club, Sister District, Social Security Works, SuperMajority, Survivors Empowered, Swing Left, Town Hall Project, UAW, UltraViolet, United Farm Workers, United We Dream, Voto Latino, VoteVets, and Women's March Bay Area.

To everyone who helped flip the House, thank you for the visionary leadership of Speaker Nancy Pelosi; Leader Steny Hoyer; Whip James Clyburn; Assistant Speaker Ben Ray Luján; Caucus Chair Hakeem Jeffries; Vice Chair Katherine Clark; DCCC Chair Cheri Bustos; Steering and Policy CoChairs Rosa DeLauro, Barbara Lee, and Eric Swalwell; Communications Chair David Cicilline and CoChairs Matt Cartwright, Debbie Dingell, and Ted Lieu; and Leadership Caucus Reps Jamie Raskin, Katie Hill, and Joe Neguse.

To all the women who marched, ran, and won for Congress in 2018, you are making history and progress: thank you Congresswomen Alma Adams, Cindy Axne, Nanette Barragán, Karen Bass, Joyce Beatty, Lisa Blunt Rochester, Suzanne Bonamici, Julia Brownley, Cheri Bustos, Kathy Castor, Judy Chu, Katherine Clark, Yvette Clarke, Angie Craig, Sharice Davids, Susan Davis, Madeleine Dean, Rosa DeLauro, Diana DeGette, Suzan DelBene, Val Demings, Debbie Dingell, Veronica Escobar, Anna Eshoo, Abby Finkenauer, Lois Frankel, Marcia Fudge, Tulsi Gabbard, Sylvia Garcia, Deb Haaland, Jahana Hayes, Katie Hill, Kendra Horn, Chrissy Houlihan, Pramila Jayapal, Eddie Bernice Johnson, Marcy Kaptur, Robin Kelly, Ann Kirkpatrick, Annie McLane Kuster, Brenda Lawrence, Barbara Lee, Susie Lee, Sheila Jackson Lee, Zoe Lofgren, Nita Lowey, Elaine Luria, Carolyn Maloney, Doris Matsui, Lucy McBath, Betty McCollum, Grace Meng, Gwen Moore, Debbie Mucarsel-Powell, Stephanie Murphy, Grace Napolitano, Alexandria Ocasio-Cortez, Ilhan Omar, Elizabeth "Lizzie" Pannill Fletcher, Nancy Pelosi, Chellie Pingree, Katie Porter, Ayanna Pressley, Kathleen Rice, Lucille Roybal-Allard, Linda Sanchez, Mary Gay Scanlon, Jan Schakowsky, Kim Schrier, Terri Sewell, Donna Shalala, Mikie Sherrill, Elissa Slotkin, Abigail Spanberger, Jackie Speier, Haley Stevens, Dina Titus, Rashida Tlaib, Norma Torres, Xochitl Torres Small, Lori Trahan, Lauren Underwood, Nadia Velazquez, Debbie Wasserman Schultz, Bonnie Watson Coleman, Jennifer

Wexton, Susan Wild, Frederick Wilson as well as delegates Eleanor Holmes-Norton and Stacey Plaskett.

To my editor Julie Ganz and the Skyhorse team and my three readers—my toughest critic (Alexandra), kindest critic (Peter), and most knowledgeable campaign critic (Jorge)— thank you for shaping the recollections into touchstones.

The best part of writing the book was remembering the moments Nancy built into movements; reflecting on every time she confounded critics, beat the odds, and inspired Democrats to progress. Tapping out notes on my phone late into the night with Bella snoozing softly nearby, I often thought of the little girl in Baltimore raised to believe in public service as a noble calling who built a movement with grace and grit and inspires us every day to be part of something larger than ourselves. Tonight as I finish, a pillow catches my eye—a baby gift from Anna Eshoo to Bella, embroidered with the message "When All Else Fails, Ask Mimi." I hope that reading this book gave you some of the answers she would.